Gold EXPERIENCE

A1

Pre-Key for Schools

Vocabulary and Grammar Workbook

Lucy Frino

Contents

	Hello!	4
01	My space	8
02	My week	14
	Revision Units 1 – 2	20
03	Wild animals	22
04	Around town	28
	Revision Units 3 – 4	34
05	Media magic	36
06	Fantastic food	42
	Revision Units 5 – 6	48
07	Life in the past	50
08	Young people, big ideas!	56
	Revision Units 7 – 8	62
09	Head to toe	64
10	Summer's here	70
	Revision Units 9 – 10	76

Hello!

VOCABULARY
Family words; Countries

1 Match (1–7) with (a–g) to make sentences.

1 My name's — d Isabel.
2 I'm — a eleven.
3 My sister — b are you?
4 We're from — c is fourteen.
5 Nice to — e Spain.
6 What's your — f meet you.
7 How old — g name?

2 Find and write eight family words.

c	o	u	s	i	n	u	s	m	u	m
a	u	n	w	r	c	o	u	s	n	u
p	i	a	d	a	d	s	a	o	c	t
o	b	v	a	n	t	c	i	g	l	h
g	r	a	n	d	m	o	t	h	e	r
r	o	f	h	f	l	u	w	o	h	i
a	t	g	r	a	w	s	y	d	c	k
c	h	h	z	t	e	i	n	a	v	e
f	e	u	i	h	f	n	o	m	u	p
e	r	c	l	e	l	i	t	o	j	n
r	a	n	d	r	o	a	u	n	t	r

1 mum
2 ....
3 ....
4 ....
5 ....
6 ....
7 ....
8 ....

3 Look at the photos of Mia's family. Complete the sentences with these words.

aunt   brother   cousin   dad
grandparents   ~~mum~~   uncle

This is me and my 1) **mum**, Annie. And this is my 2) .... He's 10.
Here's my 3) ...., Ewan. In this photo he's with my 4) ...., Ava and George.
This is my 5) ...., Scott and my 6) ...., Jessica. They're with my 7) ...., Rob. He's five.

4 Rearrange the letters to make countries.

1 insap — S **pain**
2 anich — C ....
3 tkyure — T ....
4 dplano — P ....
5 tiiarbn — B ....
6 saliautra — A ....

5 Complete the table with these words.

~~bag~~   basketball   cat   football   mouse
picture   ruler   swimming   dog

objects	sports	animals
1)	4)	7) ....
2) bag	5)	8) ....
3)	6)	9) ....

4 GOLD EXPERIENCE

READING

1 Read about Ala and Luke. Match (1–6) with the answers (a–f) to make sentences about Ala and Luke's families.

Hi! I'm Ala Nawrocka and I'm from Poland. I'm 14 years old. My brother's name is Victor. He's 16. This is a photo of us. My cousin, Martyn, is here too.

Hi, Ala! Nice to meet you! My name's Luke and I'm 12. I'm from Britain. This is a photo of me and my two sisters, Ruby and Hayley. They're 15. They're twins!

1 Hayley and Ruby   a is Ala's cousin.
2 Ala   b is from Britain.
3 Ruby   c is Ala's brother.
4 Martyn   d are Luke's sisters.
5 Luke   e is 14.
6 Victor   f is 12 years old.

2 Read about Ala and Luke again. Are the sentences (1–8) true (T) or false (F)?

1 Ala is from Poland. _T_
2 Ruby and Heidi are Luke's sisters. ___
3 Ruby is 18 years old. ___
4 Victor isn't 16 years old. ___
5 Hayley is a twin. ___
6 Three children are in Ala's photo. ___
7 Ruby and Hayley aren't from Poland. ___
8 Ala is Victor's sister. ___

GRAMMAR
Present simple with *is/are*

1 Choose the correct answer, A, B or C.

1 This ___is___ my cousin. He's eighteen.
   A are   **B is**   C be
2 My sisters _____ ten and nineteen.
   A are   B is   C be
3 Rafal _____ from Poland.
   A 'm   B 're   C 's
4 That _____ my dog.
   A aren't   B isn't   C am not
5 Joshua and Lily _____ from Britain.
   A aren't   B isn't   C is not
6 Here _____ our cats, Michel and Martha.
   A is   B are   C this

2 Put the words in the correct order to make questions.

1 name? / 's / your / What
   What's your name?
2 you? / are / old / How
3 colour? / favourite / your / What / 's
4 favourite / 's / singer? / your / Who
5 your / What / TV / favourite / 's / channel?
6 Is / this / sister's / your / bag?

3 Match the questions with these positive (+) or negative (–) short answers.

~~No, he isn't.~~   No, it isn't.   Yes, they are.
Yes, it is.   Yes, he is.   No, she isn't.
Yes, I am.   No, they aren't.

1 Is Sergio from Malawi? (–)   _No, he isn't._
2 Is Maria from Turkey? (–)
3 Is Paul from the USA? (+)
4 Are you from Britain? (+)
5 Is this Annabelle's book? (+)
6 Is this Celia's pen? (–)
7 Are these Luca's pencils? (+)
8 Are these red pens? (–)

4 Match the pets with the people. Make sentences.

1 Carmen **2** Tom **3** Georgina

4 Yuri **5** Natalie **6** John

A *3   These are Georgina's cats.*
B ....
C ....
D ....
E ....
F ....

5 Make sentences. Use *that* or *those*.

1 Elaine / pictures
   Those are Elaine's pictures.

2 Daniel / ruler

3 Amelia / dog

4 my cousin / pens

5 my mum / sister

6 Josef / books

LISTENING

1 🔊 S.1 **Listen to Vicky and Tom talking. Choose the correct answer.**

1 Vicky's favourite animal is a *cat/dog/mouse*.
2 Vicky's favourite sport is *basketball/football/swimming*.
3 Vicky's favourite TV programme is *My Brother/The X Factor/My Family*.
4 Vicky's favourite singer is *Belinda/Juanes/Paulina Rubio*.
5 Vicky's favourite song is *Be Free/See a Little Light/Angel*.
6 Vicky's favourite colour is *black/blue/purple*.

2 🔊 S.2 **Listen again and complete the sentences with one word in each space.**

1 Vicky: My dog's name _____*is*_____ Rosa.
2 Tom: What's your favourite _____?
   Vicky: Basketball is my favourite.
3 Vicky: I like _____ .
4 Tom: I _____ like *My Family*.
5 Vicky: Belinda is _____ Mexico.
6 Vicky: *Angel* is Belinda's _____ .
7 Vicky: My favourite colour _____ purple.
8 Vicky: My favourite colour is _____ .

SPEAKING SKILLS

1 Choose the correct response to the questions, A, B or C.

1. What's your name?
   A Why?
   B I'm 13.
   C Harry.
2. How old are you?
   A I'm 12 years old.
   B I'm fine thanks.
   C He's 12 years old.
3. This is my mum.
   A Nice to meet you.
   B How old are you?
   C Is she?
4. Are you from Italy?
   A No, they aren't.
   B No, I'm not.
   C No, it isn't.
5. What's your favourite team?
   A Football
   B Juventus
   C Five
6. Is this your bag?
   A Yes, she is.
   B Yes, there is.
   C Yes, it is.
7. Are these Omar's pens?
   A Yes, they are.
   B Yes, it is.
   C Yes, these.

2 Put the lines of the conversation in the correct order (1–8).

Sally: Do you like the music channel? _1_
Karl: I like Chris Martin from Coldplay. ___
Sally: Who's your favourite singer? ___
Sally: Why do you like *Yellow*? ___
Sally: Yes. Coldplay are great. ___
Karl: Yes, I do. It's my favourite TV channel. ___
Karl: I like their song *Yellow*. ___
Karl: I don't know. But yellow is my favourite colour! ___

WRITING

1 Look at the photo of Claudia and her family. Choose the correct words.

❝ ¹*I/This* is my family. My grandparents' ²*name/names* are Leonardo and Giacinta. In this photo they ³*is/are* with their five children. I'm Claudia. I'm 14 ⁴*with/and* my brother Ricardo is 12. My mum's name ⁵*'re/'s* Loretta. She's ⁶*from/for Italy*. My dad ⁷*isn't/is* from Italy. He's from Britain. ⁸*Here's/His* name is Jack. ❞

2 Put the words in the correct order to make sentences.

1. is Marco Ecuador from.
   Marco is from Ecuador.
2. old He's years 13.

3. His is sport football favourite.

4. cousins His football, too like.

5. is favourite team Olmedo Their.

6. dog's is Marco's Bilbo name.

7. colour is favourite blue Marco's.

8. the like I channel music.

01 My space

VOCABULARY
Things in a room

1 Match the picture with these words.

> clock   computer   cupboard   curtains
> desk   electric guitar   shelf

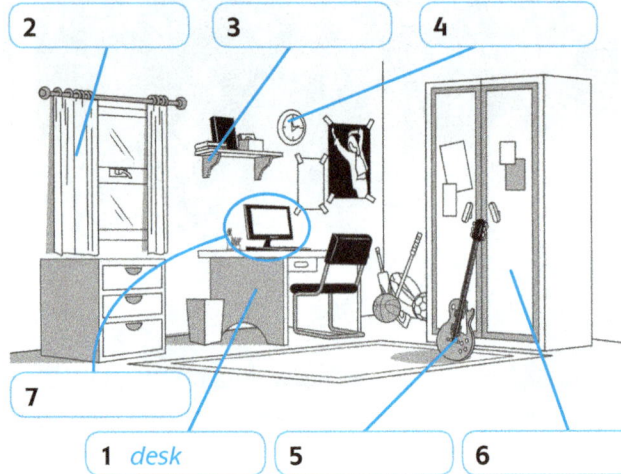

1 desk   2 ___   3 ___   4 ___   5 ___   6 ___   7 ___

2 Read the clues. Complete the crossword puzzle.

1 It's above my computer. It's a l _i_ g _h_ _t_ .
2 I read it. It's a c___ ___ ___ c.
3 It's under my desk. It's my b___ n.
4 I sit on it. It's a c___ sh___ ___ .
5 They're next to the window. They're c___ ta___ ns.
6 It's near my desk. I sit on it. It's my ch___ ___ ___ .

Crossword:
1 L
  I
  G
  H
  T

3 Rearrange the letters to make things in a room.

1 oclkc — _clock_
2 vlesshe — ___
3 trespo — ___
4 aiurtcns — ___
5 iemobl ohpen — ___
6 scimu yerpal — ___

4 Complete the table with these words. There are two words you do not need.

> ~~comic~~   cupboard   curtains   electric guitar
> mobile phone
> music player   noticeboard   poster

Read	Listen to
1) _comic_	4) ___
2) ___	5) ___
3) ___	6) ___

5 Look at the pictures. Complete the sentences.

1 The comic is ___in___ the bin.
2 The mouse is ___ the cupboard.
3 The mobile phone is ___ the desk.
4 The clock is ___ the shelf.

GOLD EXPERIENCE

01 My space

READING

1 Read the text about Callum's house. Are the sentences true for Callum's room (C), Lexie's room (L) or Mum and Dad's room (MD)?

1 There's a blue bed. _C_
2 There are books on the shelves. ____
3 The chair is pink. ____
4 There's a poster of a pop star on the wall. ____
5 There's a TV. ____
6 The curtains are yellow. ____

> **My house**
> by Callum MacKenzie
>
> My bedroom is my favourite room. There's a blue bed, a big cupboard and a small table next to the bed. My CDs are on the shelves next to the window and my music player is on the floor. I like the big window and the yellow curtains.
>   I've got a sister called Lexie. Her room is very pink. There's a pink bed, a pink desk and a pink chair. There's a pink bin under the desk, too! I don't like the poster of Justin Bieber in Lexie's room. It's on the wall above her bed.
>   In my mum and dad's bedroom there's a big bed. There are two chairs and there are lots of books on the shelves. There's also a small TV on the wall.

2 Read the text again. Complete the sentences with these words.

> under   on   isn't   aren't   ~~next to~~   is

1 Callum's table is _next to_ his bed.
2 Callum's music player is ____ the floor.
3 There's a bin ____ the desk in Lexie's room.
4 Lexie's room ____ blue.
5 There ____ any CDs in mum and dad's room.
6 The TV in mum and dad's room ____ small.

GRAMMAR
There is/There are

1 Match (1–6) with (a–f) to make sentences about Mirek's bedroom.

1 There's a — a electric guitar.
2 There are some books b on the shelf.
3 There aren't any c cupboard.
4 There's a d clock on the desk.
5 There isn't an e curtains.
6 There isn't anything in the f desk next to the bed.

2 Make positive (+) or negative (-) short answers. Use *Yes, there is/Yes, there are*, or *No, there isn't/No, there aren't*.

1 Is there a bin? (-) _No, there isn't._
2 Are there any cushions? (+) ____
3 Is there a shelf? (+) ____
4 Are there any lights? (-) ____
5 Is there a noticeboard? (-) ____
6 Is there a cupboard? (+) ____

3 Complete the text with these words.

> a   any   are   aren't   's ×2   some

Hi, I'm Hilaria. There' 1) _'s_ my school bag, near the door. What's in my bag? There 2) ____ some trainers and there's 3) ____ football. I love football. There aren't 4) ____ pencils but there are 5) ____ pens. There 6) ____ a notebook for my English homework. There's my mobile phone. There 7) ____ any pictures on it at the moment.

4 Make questions. Use *Is there* or *Are there*.

1 pictures / bedroom
   Are there any pictures in your bedroom?
2 pencil case / bag
3 books / shelves
4 poster / bedroom
5 mobile phone / bag
6 trainers / cupboard

VOCABULARY
The home

1 Choose the correct words.

1. kitchen / bathroom / <u>garage</u>
2. bathroom / bedroom / balcony
3. garden / lift / balcony
4. living room / dining room / bedroom
5. lift / balcony / living room
6. bathroom / stairs / kitchen

2 Match the picture with these words.

<s>bathroom</s>   bedroom   downstairs   kitchen
living room   stairs   upstairs

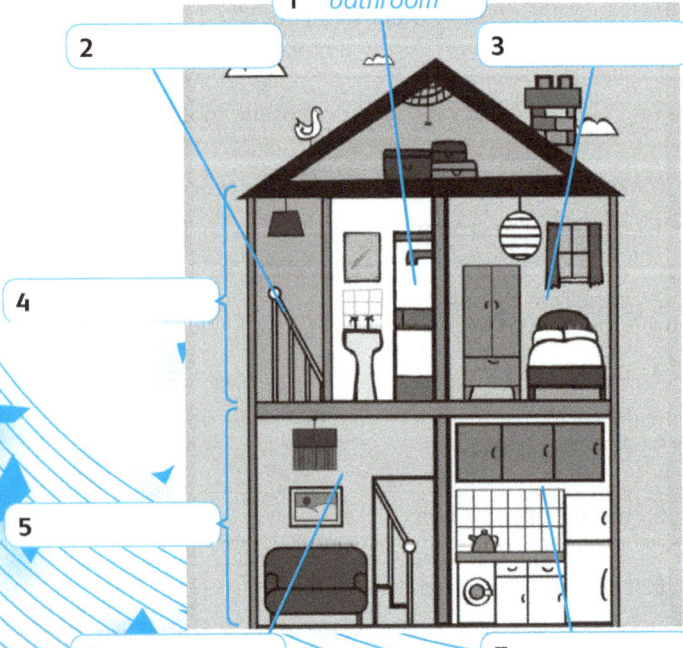

1. bathroom
2.
3.
4.
5.
6.
7.

3 Choose the correct answer, A, B or C.

1. I like cooking. Yum! The ___kitchen___ is my favourite room.
   A bathroom   **B kitchen**   C balcony
2. There's a _____ next to my house. My mum and dad's car is there.
   A balcony   B lift   C garage
3. I'm from Spain. There's a _____ outside my flat.
   A balcony   B bedroom   C stairs
4. I'm from Australia. There's a swimming pool in my _____.
   A bedroom   B garden   C kitchen
5. There are two _____ in my house – one for my mum and dad, and one for me and my brothers and sisters.
   A stairs   B bathrooms   C downstairs
6. We like parties. There is a big _____ in our house, with a table and ten chairs.
   A dining room   B bathroom   C garage
7. I have a desk in my _____ so I can do my homework.
   A bedroom   B stairs   C balcony

4 Complete the text with these words.

bedrooms   garage   garden   lift
living room   <s>swimming pool</s>

Hi, welcome to my house! There's a very big 1) _swimming pool_ in the 2) _____. Swimming is cool. Downstairs is my favourite room – the 3) _____. My piano and my guitar are there. There aren't any stairs in my house – there's a special 4) _____. There are ten 5) _____ upstairs, yes, ten! They're for all my friends. There's a 6) _____ under the house, with six cars inside. Isn't it fantastic?

01 My space

LISTENING

1 🔊 **1.1 Listen and choose the correct photograph.**

1 A 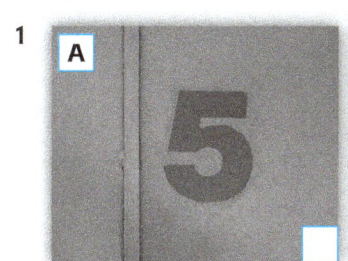 B

2 A 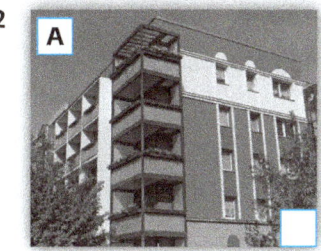 B

3 A 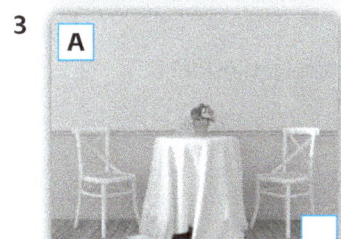 B

4 A 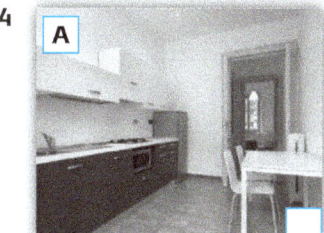 B

5 A  B

6 A 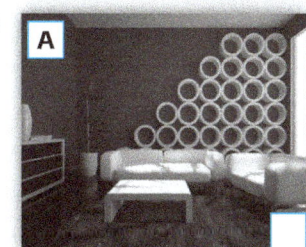 B

2 🔊 **1.2 Listen again and choose the correct answer.**

1 Silvia's from *France/Spain/Britain*.
2 There are cars *outside/inside/under* Silvia's apartment.
3 Silvia's dining room has got *red/yellow/white* walls.
4 Silvia's kitchen hasn't got a *table/TV/chair* in it.
5 Silvia and her sister have got a *computer/TV/electric guitar* in their room.
6 The window in the living room is *small/black/big*.

GRAMMAR
have got

1 Choose the correct words.

1 Angela*'s/'ve* got lots of books in her bedroom.
2 My house *has/hasn't* got any stairs inside.
3 The living room*'s/'ve* got a beautiful light.
4 My dogs *has/have* got a cushion in the kitchen.
5 The windows in the bedroom *has/have* got green curtains.
6 Juan Manuel*'s/'ve* got a big music player in his bedroom.
7 We*'ve/'s* got six chairs in the living room.
8 My bedroom *have/has* got lots of pictures on the wall.

2 Look at Fiona's bedroom. Make sentences.

1 *There's a desk and a chair.*
2 ....
3 ....
4 ....

11

3 **Complete the interview with one word in each space. Use contractions.**

Man: Good morning, Eve. You 1) _'ve_ got a fantastic house.
Eve: Thank you. It's an old windmill.
Man: How many rooms 2) _____ it got?
Eve: It 3) _____ got seven rooms. One of the bedrooms is downstairs and it's 4) _____ a living room upstairs.
Man: And how many stairs 5) _____ your house got?
Eve: I don't know! I think 6) _____ 's got 50.
Man: Have 7) _____ got a big bedroom?
Eve: No, I 8) _____. My bedroom is round and it's got small windows, but I love it!

4 **Read the answers. Make questions.**

1 your / a / flat / Has / got / balcony?
Yes, it has.
   Has your flat got a balcony?

2 your / garden? / house / got / Has / a
No, it hasn't.

3 Have / house? / got / stairs / you / your / in
Yes, we have. There are 14 stairs.

4 pets? / got / you / Have
No, I haven't. I don't like animals.

5 apartment / your / lift? / Has / got / a
Yes, it has.

6 Have / a / garage / you / your / outside / house? / got
No, we haven't. We haven't got a car.

5 **Choose the correct answer, A, B or C.**

1 Has your bedroom got yellow walls?
  A Yes, I have.
  (B) Yes, it has.
  C Yes, we have.
2 Has the flat got a lift?
  A No, it hasn't.
  B No, I haven't.
  C Yes, it is.
3 Have your grandparents got a garden?
  A No, they aren't.
  B Yes, it is.
  C Yes, they have.
4 Have you got a shower in your bathroom?
  A Yes, we have.
  B No, it isn't.
  C No, you haven't.
5 Has Mariano got a desk in his bedroom?
  A No, I haven't.
  B Yes, he has.
  C Yes, there is.
6 Has the cupboard got shelves inside?
  A Yes, there are.
  B Yes, it has.
  C Yes, they have.

6 **Make positive (+) or negative (−) short answers.**

1 Has your house got a garden? (+)
   Yes, it has.
2 Have you got a dining room? (+)

3 Have you got a swimming pool? (−)

4 Has your house got a big kitchen? (+)

5 Has your house got stairs? (−)

6 Have you got three bedrooms in your house? (−)

7 Has your bathroom got a shower? (+)

01 My space

SPEAKING SKILLS

1 Read parts of seven telephone conversations and choose the best response, A, B or C.

1 Hello?
  A Goodbye.
  B Hello. It's Ariana.
  C OK.

2 Is Yana there?
  A She's Yana.
  B Yes, she is.
  C Yes, there is.

3 Just a minute.
  A Hello?
  B No, thanks.
  C OK.

4 It's Dario here.
  A No, it isn't.
  B Oh, hello, Dario.
  C Oh, hello, Cristiano.

5 Have you got my history book?
  A Yes, it is.
  B Yes. It's on my shelf.
  C No, you haven't.

6 Thanks, Patricia.
  A Thanks.
  B That's good.
  C That's OK.

7 Bye!
  A Bye!
  B Hello.
  C OK.

2 Complete the telephone conversation with the words below.

> a   Bye   ~~here~~   Hi   It's   Thanks   there   you

Richard: Hello, Mr Tims. It's Richard ¹ _here_ . Is Zak ² _____ , please?
Mr Tims: Yes, he's in his bedroom. Just ³ _____ minute.
Zak: Hi? Richard?
Richard: ⁴ _____ , Zak. I can't find my mobile phone. Have ⁵ _____ got it?
Zak: I'm not sure … Oh yes. ⁶ _____ in my bag.
Richard: Oh good. ⁷ _____ , Zak.
Zak: That's OK. Bye, Richard!
Richard: ⁸ _____ . See you tomorrow.

WRITING

1 Choose the correct word to complete the sentences.

1 Here are some cinema *tickets*/*postcards*.
2 This is a photo *of*/*about* me.
3 Basketball is my favourite *sport*/*animal*.
4 These are my birthday *cards*/*tickets*.
5 What's your mobile *number*/*photo*?
6 This is a postcard *from*/*of* my sister.

2 Look at the postcards and photos from Maria's bedroom wall. Match A–F with sentences 1–6.

1 This is a photo of my brother. _B_
2 Here's a photo of my grandparents and my mum. ___
3 That's a postcard from my uncle in France. ___
4 That ticket is for my favourite band. ___
5 This is a postcard of a beach. ___
6 I've got a cat. ___

3 Choose six things to put on your wall. Write six short sentences about the photos, pictures and tickets. Make sure there are capital letters for names of people and places, and at the start of sentences.

02 My week

VOCABULARY
Days of the week; Daily activities

1 Number the days of the week in the correct order, (1–7).

```
___ Friday    _1_ Monday    ___ Saturday
___ Sunday    ___ Thursday
___ Tuesday   ___ Wednesday
```

2 Match (1–8) with (a–h) to make phrases about your day.

1	go to	a	homework
2	have a	b	the shops
3	do my	c	shower
4	get	d	my friends
5	meet	e	TV
6	play	f	to my friends
7	watch	g	computer games
8	talk	h	up

3 Put the words in the correct order.

1 in / dressed / morning. / I / get / the
   I get dressed in the morning.

2 have / in / shower / the / I / / a / morning.
   _____

3 breakfast / with / my / parents. / have / I
   _____

4 I / evening. / watch / in / the / TV
   _____

5 to / shops / Wednesday. / I / the / go / on
   _____

6 lunch / have / afternoon. / the / I / in
   _____

7 meet / friends / Saturday. / I / my / on
   _____

4 Look at the pictures. Complete the sentences.

1 I _do_ _my_ _homework_ in the afternoon.
2 I _____ my _____ on Tuesday.
3 I _____ in the evening.
4 I _____ my grandmother on Thursday.
5 I _____ on Saturday.
6 I _____ with my family on Sunday.

READING

1 Read Zarek's online post on page 15 and complete the table.

Name of the language school	1 _First English Language School_
Number of students at the school	2
How old the students in Zarek's class are, 14 and	3
Number of students from Poland	4
School day starts at half past	5
School day ends at half past	6
Free days Saturday and	7

14 GOLD EXPERIENCE

02 My week

Zarek in London!
I'm in London at the First English Language School. There are 60 students here at the school. Four of the students in my class are from Poland and four are from Spain. There are two girls from Mexico and three boys from China, too. We're all 14 or 15 years old and we're one big happy family. This is a photo of me with some of my class.

The lessons start at 8.30 in the morning. We don't have lessons in the afternoon. We play games or sport. At 4.30 we go home to our British 'families'. They look after us while we're in England. In the evening I do my homework, watch TV or play computer games with the brother from the family. He's 13 and his name is Cameron.

There aren't any lessons on Saturday and Sunday. On Saturday I meet my friends from the school and we go to the shops. On Sunday I go with Cameron to see his grandparents in Essex and I talk to my sister and my parents in Poland on the computer.

2 Read Zarek's online post again. Choose the correct answer, A, B or C.

1 Zarek is 14.
   A true
   B false
   (C) don't know
2 Zarek goes home at 5.30.
   A true
   B false
   C don't know
3 There are three people in Zarek's English 'family'.
   A true
   B false
   C don't know
4 Zarek doesn't play with Cameron.
   A true
   B false
   C don't know

5 Zarek goes to the shops on Saturday.
   A true
   B false
   C don't know
6 Cameron's grandparents are in Essex.
   A true
   B false
   C don't know
7 Zarek has a brother.
   A true
   B false
   C don't know
8 Zarek's from Spain.
   A true
   B false
   C don't know

GRAMMAR
Present simple for regular activities

1 Choose the correct words.

Life at St Edmund's Music School

School subjects
The school is a music school but the students 1) *has/have* other subjects too, for example, art, geography and science.

The school day
Students at the school 2) *gets up/get up* at 6.30 in the morning. They 3) *has/have* lunch at 12.30. The school day 4) *end/ends* at 7.00 in the evening.

The school week
Students 5) *doesn't/don't* have music classes on Saturday. The school 6) *don't/doesn't* open on Sunday.

2 Clara is a student at the music school. Complete what she says with these words.

don't ×2   get   have ×3   play   ~~start~~

" I 1) _start_ the day at 6.30. First I 2) _____ dressed and I 3) _____ breakfast. I 4) _____ watch TV in the morning, there are music lessons! I 5) _____ the piano in music class and then 6) _____ lunch at 12.00. I 7) _____ play music all day – in the afternoon we 8) _____ other subjects. I do my homework in the evening and the day ends at 9.30 at night. "

15

3 **Choose the correct answer, A or B.**

1 Students at the school ____play____ the guitar in music classes.
  A play   B plays
2 They _____ dressed in the morning.
  A get   B gets
3 The students _____ computer games at school.
  A doesn't play   B don't play
4 Ethan _____ breakfast at 7.00 in the morning.
  A has   B have
5 They _____ science in the afternoons.
  A has   B have
6 My sister _____ TV in the afternoon.
  A doesn't watch   B don't watch
7 Susan _____ to her friends in the evening.
  A talk   B talks
8 Stefano _____ to school on Saturday.
  A go   B goes

4 **Rewrite the sentences in the negative form.**

1 Sam gets up at 6.00 in the morning.
  Sam doesn't get up at 6.00 in the morning.
2 His school day starts at 7.00.
  _____
3 Sam's mum and dad watch TV in the afternoon.
  _____
4 Sam's grandmother goes to the shops on Monday.
  _____
5 Sam's sister plays the guitar.
  _____
6 Sam and his sister go to the beach on Sunday.
  _____

VOCABULARY
Free time activities

1 **Choose the correct phrase.**

1 have singing lessons/ have swimming lessons
2 play volleyball/play computer games

3 play computer games/ play the guitar
4 play card games/play football

2 **Complete the table with these phrases.**

a party   fun   the drums   ~~to the beach~~
to the cinema   volleyball

go	have	play
1) *to the beach*	3) _____	5) _____
2) _____	4) _____	6) _____

3 **Find and write eight months of the year.**

d	j	a	n	u	a	r	y	a
e	w	u	o	s	j	s	c	o
c	t	s	v	d	u	y	e	c
e	o	a	e	i	l	h	o	t
m	r	p	m	u	y	e	l	o
b	e	r	b	o	c	a	g	b
e	n	i	e	a	m	a	y	e
r	p	l	r	s	y	i	b	r
a	a	u	g	u	s	t	e	d

1 *January*   5 _____
2 _____   6 _____
3 _____   7 _____
4 _____   8 _____

02 My week

4 Rearrange the letters to make months.

1 rbootce — *October*
2 cramh — ....
3 cebdmere — ....
4 raubefry — ....
5 neuj — ....
6 petmesber — ....

5 Match the pictures with these words.

~~history~~   science   art   maths
geography   English

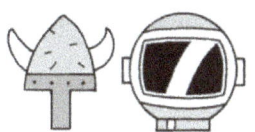
1 *history*

2 ....

3 ....

4 ....

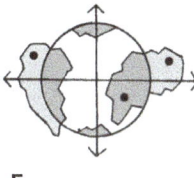
5 ....

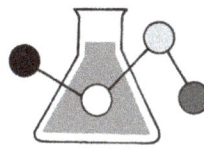
6 ....

6 Choose the correct words.

1 I have swimming lessons *in/on/at* June.
2 I do my homework *in/on/at* Saturday.
3 I watch TV *in/on/at* 6.00.
4 We go to the cinema *in/on/at* 8.00.
5 We play volleyball *in/on/at* July.
6 I meet my friends *in/on/at* Friday.

7 Complete the sentences with *in*, *on* or *at*.

1 I get up _at_ 8.00.
2 It is the start of the week .... Monday.
3 We have singing lessons .... April.
4 Ellen goes to the beach .... August.
5 I have English class .... 10.00.
6 My cousins play football .... Saturday.
7 Karl has lunch .... 1.00.

LISTENING

1 🔊 2.1 Listen to the conversation between Alex and his cousin Briony. Choose the correct words.

1 Journey to school: Briony *walks*/*doesn't* walk to school
2 Journey time: *15/25* minutes
3 Briony's favourite subjects: English and *history/geography*
4 Day Briony has singing lessons: *Monday/Wednesday*
5 Sports Briony plays: *basketball/football* and volleyball
6 Briony does her homework: *before/after* dinner

2 🔊 2.2 Listen to the conversation again. Choose the correct answer, A, B or C.

1 Does Briony like her new school?
   (A) Yes, she does.
   B She doesn't know.
   C No, she doesn't.

2 What time does she go to school in the morning?
   A At 9.30.
   B At 8.30.
   C 15 minutes.

3 Does Maria go to school with Briony?
   A Not every day.
   B Yes, she does.
   C No, she doesn't.

4 Does Briony have lunch at school?
   A Not today.
   B Yes, she does.
   C No, she doesn't.

5 Does Briony have lessons in the afternoon?
   A No, she doesn't.
   B Yes, she does.
   C Singing lessons.

6 What time does Briony finish school?
   A 3.45
   B 3.00
   C 3.30

GRAMMAR
Present simple: questions and short answers

1 Choose *do* or *does*, then complete the questions with these verbs.

> end get up go help ~~like~~ meet play

1 *Do/Does* your best friend ___like___ football?
2 What time *do/does* you _____ in the morning?
3 *Do/Does* your sister _____ volleyball?
4 What time *do/does* your guitar lesson _____?
5 *Do/Does* you _____ to English class?
6 *Do/Does* your mother _____ with your homework?
7 What time *do/does* you _____ your friends?

2 Choose the correct answer, A, B or C.

1 Does your father have swimming lessons?
  A No, she doesn't.   B No, we don't.
  C No, he doesn't. *(circled)*
2 What time do you have English class?
  A At 10.00.   B Yes, I do.
  C No, they don't.
3 Do you and your friends go to the beach?
  A Yes, they do.   B Yes, I do.
  C Yes, we do.
4 Do your friends have a party every day?
  A No, we don't.   B No, they don't.
  C No, she doesn't.
5 Do you like science?
  A Yes, he does.   B Yes, they do.
  C Yes, I do.
6 Does your sister play the guitar?
  A Yes, she does.   B Yes, he does.
  C Yes, they do.
7 When do you go to bed?
  A In the morning.   B In March.
  C At 9.00 at night.

3 Match the questions (1–8) with the answers (a–h).

1 Do you play football?
2 Do your parents go to the cinema?
3 Do you have a brother?
4 Do you have singing lessons?
5 Does your dad play computer games?
6 Do your friends play volleyball?
7 Does your mother go to school?
8 Does your best friend study English?

a No, I don't. I like to play the guitar.
b Yes, they do. They play on Saturday.
c No, she doesn't. She's 42.
d Yes, I do. His name is Pedro.
e Yes, he does. He's in my class.
f No, he doesn't. He watches TV.
g Yes, they do. They like films.
h Yes, I do. I play on Saturday.

4 Make questions for a student in Britain.

1 do homework / every day?
  ___Do you do homework every day?___
2 when / get up / in the morning?
3 what time / have lunch?
4 watch TV / evening?
5 go / cinema / weekend?

SPEAKING SKILLS

1 Match the questions (1–7) with the answers (a–g).

1 What time do you get up for school?
2 Do you go to school with your friends?
3 Do you have English in the morning or in the afternoon?
4 Do you have science lessons on Friday?
5 Do you like maths?
6 What time do you have lunch?
7 What time do you go home?

a Yes, I do. We walk to school.
b At 3.30, when school finishes.
c No, I don't. I like history and geography.
d No, we don't. They're on Tuesday.
e At 12.30.
f In the afternoon.
g At 7.30 in the morning.

02 My week

2 Complete the conversations about Harry's school day. Choose the correct words.

1
Dad: Harry, it's eight o'clock. Let's go!
Harry: It's OK, Dad. I ¹ *start/finish/go* school at half past eight in the morning at my new school.
Dad: Oh, yes. And when do you have a break?
Harry: We ² *are/do/have* a break at eleven o'clock.
Dad: Then lunch is ³ *at/in/on* twelve o'clock?
Harry: Yes, that's right. Then we start lessons at one o'clock ⁴ *at/in/on* the afternoon.
Dad: What time do you come home? Three o'clock?
Harry: No, Dad, I come home at half ⁵ *and/past/for* three.

2
Mum: Is it maths today, Harry?
Harry: Yes, Mum. It's Tuesday. I have maths ⁶ *at/in/on* Tuesday and Thursday.
Mum: OK. Is maths your favourite subject?
Harry: Hmm, no. My favourite subject is sport.
Mum: Have you got sport today?
Harry: No, sport is on Monday ⁷ *in/and/on* Wednesday in the afternoon.
Mum: Oh, yes. What about music? Is it today?
Harry: No, my music lesson is on Friday, Mum. It ⁸ *starts/has/plays* at half past two in the afternoon.
Mum: Ah, yes. That's right.

WRITING

1 Look at the table about Karen and Ben. Complete the questions. Write two words in each space.

	Karen	Ben	Karen and Ben
Monday	singing lessons		beach (4.00)
Tuesday		guitar lessons	
Wednesday	swimming lessons		beach (4.00)
Thursday		science lessons	
Friday			volleyball (5.00)

1 **A** When _does Karen_ have swimming lessons?
  B On Wednesday.
2 **A** What _____ Karen and Ben play volleyball on Friday?
  B At five o'clock.
3 **A** _____ have singing lessons?
  B No, he doesn't.
4 **A** What does Ben do _____ ?
  B He has science lessons.
5 **A** What time do Karen and Ben _____ the beach?
  B At four o'clock.
6 **A** When does Ben have _____ ?
  B On Tuesday.
7 **A** Do Karen and Ben _____ on Friday after school?
  B Yes, they do.

2 Write questions for the answers about the English teacher, Jenny Williams. Use the prompts to help you.

1 **A** (Where/she/from?) _Where is she from?_
  B The USA.
2 **A** (How many sisters/she/got?) _____
  B Four.
3 **A** (How old/she?) _____
  B 31.
4 **A** (she/play golf?) _____
  B Yes, she does.
5 **A** (What time/she/get up?) _____
  B At 6.30 a.m.
6 **A** (What/her/favourite food?) _____
  B Pizza.

3 Make a quiz! Write six questions about your favourite singer or sports star's life. Then write the answers. Make sure you use question marks, full stops and capital letters correctly.

Revision Units 1 - 2

VOCABULARY

1 Look at the picture and rearrange the letters to make words.

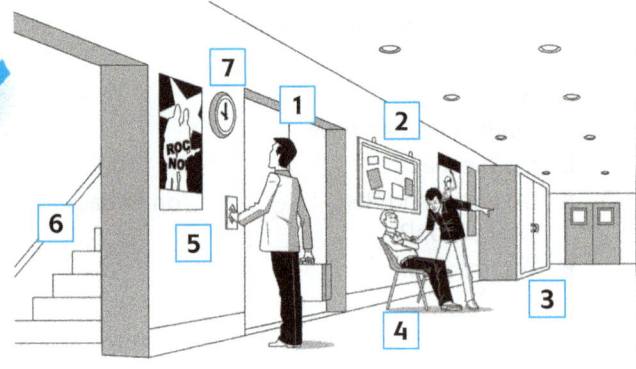

1 fitl — lift
2 brtneiooacd — ....
3 uoardpcb — ....
4 hirac — ....
5 preost — ....
6 rissta — ....
7 colck — ....

2 Choose the correct words.

1 There are *curtains/bedrooms* next to the window.
2 She plays the *guitar/mobile phone*.
3 Is your birthday in *Friday/February*?
4 The books are *on/above* the shelves.
5 I've got blue *cushions/gardens* in my bedroom.
6 My house isn't *near/next* my school.
7 Our computer is *downstairs/living room*.
8 Your bag is *between/on* the desk and the chair.

3 Put the months in order.

May, February, July, August, January, June, March, April, December, October, September, November

4 Read and choose the best answer, A, B or C.

My 1) __cousin__ Jessica is from the USA. Her mum is my 2) ____'s sister. Saturday for Jessica is different from my Saturday. She 3) ____ up at 8 o'clock and she 4) ____ to the shops. She 5) ____ lunch and then she goes to the 6) ____. In the evening she 7) ____ singing lessons. On Saturday, I 8) ____ football or computer games.

1	A	uncle	B dad	**C**	cousin
2	A	mum	B sister	C	grandmother
3	A	goes	B gets	C	plays
4	A	gets	B has	C	goes
5	A	has	B does	C	is
6	A	fun	B dinner	C	cinema
7	A	goes	B has	C	plays
8	A	play	B go	C	get

5 Look at the timetable. Complete the text with one word in each space.

Monday	Tuesday	
🎨	X+Y=	
🎨	🧪	
Lunch	Lunch	Lunch
⚛	👨‍🚀	🎨
X+Y=	📖	🎨

"Here's my school timetable. On 1) M__onday__ morning I have two 2) a_____ lessons. After lunch I have 3) g_____ and 4) m_____. On 5) _____ morning I have maths, then 6) s_____. That's my favourite subject. In the afternoon I have 7) h_____ and 8) E_____."

20 GOLD EXPERIENCE

REVISION Units 1 – 2

GRAMMAR

1 Choose the correct words.
1 There *'s/are* a swimming pool in my grandfather's garden.
2 There *isn't/aren't* a lift.
3 *Is/Are* there any shelves in your bedroom?
4 Yes, there *are/aren't*.
5 Elena *'ve/'s* got four brothers.
6 We *'ve/'s* got a music player in the living room.
7 *Has/Have* you got a pet?
8 No, I *have/haven't*.

2 Make negative sentences.
1 I / play the drums
   I don't play the drums.
2 my dad / play card games
   ....
3 there / be / cupboard / living room
   ....
4 there / be / pictures / kitchen
   ....
5 there / be / garage / downstairs
   ....
6 we / have got / dining room / our house
   ....
7 Silvia / have got / desk / her bedroom
   ....

3 Complete the questions with the correct verbs.
1 ....*Has*.... he got a TV in his bedroom?
2 .... you talk to your friends on your mobile phone?
3 .... there a bin in the living room?
4 .... Frank have lunch at school?
5 .... there electric guitars in this shop?
6 .... you got a cushion, please?
7 .... your grandparents go to the beach?
8 .... this garage got a light?

4 Make positive (+) or negative (–) short answers.
1 Do you get dressed in your bedroom? (+)
   Yes, I do.
2 I don't like lifts. Are there any stairs? (+)
   ....
3 Does your mum play computer games? (–)
   ....
4 Is there a noticeboard at your school? (+)
   ....
5 Has your house got stairs? (–)
   ....
6 Have your grandparents got a pet? (–)
   ....

5 Complete the email with these words.

| don't | ~~get up~~ | go | have ×2 | on | play |

Subject: **My school day!**

Hi Franklin,
How are you? This week's email is about my school day. At seven o'clock I 1) ....*get up*.... and 2) .... breakfast with my parents. I 3) .... to school at eight o'clock. We 4) .... English in the mornings 5) .... Monday and Wednesday. We 6) .... have swimming lessons at school. I swim at the weekend with my friends. I like volleyball. I 7) .... volleyball on Saturday. What about you?
Bye for now.
Emily

6 Complete what Katarina says with one word in each space.

View previous comments   Cancel   Share   Post

I 1) ....*'m*.... Katarina. I'm 2) .... Poland. Here's a photo 3) .... me. I've got a pet dog and my brother 4) .... got a pet cat. My dog 5) .... like the cat! I 6) .... my friends on Saturday, and on Sunday I 7) .... the guitar. I 8) .... play football. What about you?

Write a comment   Support

03 Wild animals

VOCABULARY
Animals

1 Look at the photos. Complete the crossword puzzle.

 1
 2
 3
 4
 5
 6
 7
 8

2 Complete the sentences with these animal names.

> bears   ~~camels~~   llamas   meerkats
> pandas   spiders

1 _Camels_ don't drink a lot of water.
2 _____ live in Africa. They've got four legs.
3 _____ are black and white.
4 _____ sleep in the winter.
5 _____ have got eight legs.
6 _____ live in Ecuador. They aren't small.

3 Complete the table with these animals.

> camels   goats   meerkats   ~~scorpions~~
> sharks   whales

They sleep under ground	They work with people	They live in the sea
1) _scorpions_	3) _____	5) _____
2) _____	4) _____	6) _____

4 Put the words about these animals in the correct order.

1 black bear — lives / in / It / the USA.
   It lives in the USA.
2 panda — eats / plants. / It
3 parrot — has / got / two / legs. / It
4 snake — It / any / got / hasn't / legs.
5 meerkat — has / lots / Its / home / got / of / rooms.
6 scorpion — small / dangerous. / is / It / and

Crossword answer: KANGAROO

03 Wild animals

READING

1 Read the article. Choose the correct words or phrases.

BAT FACTS

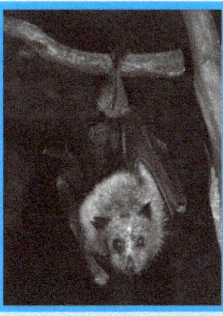

About bats
Bats are very interesting animals. They sleep in the day and they come out at night and look for food. Bats don't usually see in colour. They only see in black and white.

Their food
Bats often eat insects. A brown bat eats 600 insects in one hour! Bats also eat fruit and meat and they drink from flowers. Some bats eat fish.

Their home
Bats sleep and hide in caves or forests. They're safe there from other animals. People sometimes make houses for bats in their gardens.

The babies
Mother bats usually have one baby in a year. Baby bats are called pups. They drink milk from their mother.

Bats sing!
Bats sometimes make noises or 'sing'. They sing to find the other bats in their family.

1 Bats sleep in the *evening/day/night*.
2 Bats often eat *insects/eggs/plants*.
3 Bats sleep in trees or *caves/in rivers or seas/under the ground*.
4 Bat houses are sometimes *in people's kitchens/in people's living rooms/in people's gardens*.
5 Baby bats drink *orange juice/water/milk*.
6 Bats live in *families/big groups/twos*.

2 Read the article again. Complete the sentences with these words.

> near   have   ~~interesting~~   are   night
> black   sing

1 Bats are very *interesting* animals.
2 They come out at _____ .
3 They see in _____ and white.
4 Some bats live _____ rivers or the sea.
5 Bats _____ safe in caves or forests.
6 Bats usually _____ one baby.
7 Bats _____ to find their family.

GRAMMAR
Adverbs of frequency

1 Match (1–6) with (a–f) to make sentences.

1 Pandas — a don't often drink.
2 Dolphins — b never eat birds.
3 Brown bears   c are often very funny.
4 Camels   d sometimes play games in the water.
5 Meerkats   e sometimes talk.
6 Parrots   f usually sleep in the cold months.

2 Read the article. Choose the correct answer, A, B or C.

Subject: Wild kangaroos

Wild kangaroos 1) *always* live in Australia. They usually 2) _____ in groups of about ten. A group of kangaroos is called a mob. They aren't 3) _____ brown. Some kangaroos are grey. Kangaroos only eat plants. They 4) _____ eat spiders or beetles. Kangaroos aren't usually dangerous, but they 5) _____ attack people. Cars are dangerous for kangaroos. In Australia, there 6) _____ often 'kangaroo crossing' signs next to the roads.

1 **A** always   B never   C don't
2 A have   B live   C talk
3 A never   B always   C sometimes
4 A never   B always   C sometimes
5 A always   B sometimes   C often
6 A have   B do   C are

A kangaroo crossing sign

3 Rewrite the sentences. Put the adverb in brackets in the correct place.

1 Giorgio gets up at eight. (always)
   Giorgio always gets up at eight.
2 He doesn't go to the shops. (usually)
3 He meets his friends on Saturday. (sometimes)
4 He's happy. (usually)
5 Giorgio watches TV. (never)
6 He doesn't go to the cinema. (often)
7 He plays football. (often)
8 His brother is with him. (usually)

4 Put the words in the correct order.

1 usually / has / Kasia / her / got / mobile phone.
   Kasia has usually got her mobile phone.
2 She / singing / sometimes / lessons. / has
3 doesn't / play / usually / She / volleyball.
4 drums. / the / never / She / plays
5 often / She / play / games. / computer / doesn't
6 does / usually / her / the / evening. / She / homework / in

VOCABULARY
The world around us

1 Choose the correct words.

1 Parrots usually live in a *river/jungle*.
2 Fish always live in *water/a cave*.
3 Pandas usually live *in a river/on a mountain*.
4 Camels live in *the sea/a desert*.
5 Bats often live in a *cave/desert*.
6 Spiders sometimes live in *the sea/a forest*.
7 Sharks never live in *lakes/the sea*.
8 Kangaroos always live *in rivers/on land*.

2 Complete the words. Use the photos to help you.

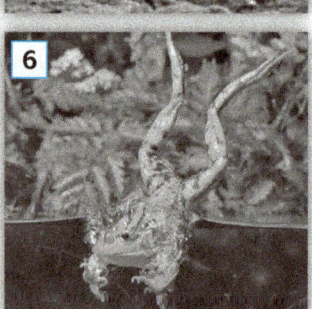

1 h _o_ _p_
2 r_____ _____
3 f_____ _____
4 w_____ _____
5 s_____ _____
6 j_____ _____

24 GOLD EXPERIENCE

03 Wild animals

3 Are the sentences (1–6) true (T) or false (F)?
1 Whales jump.   *F*
2 Sharks swim.   ____
3 Parrots fly.   ____
4 Goats walk.   ____
5 Dolphins hop.   ____
6 Bats run.   ____

4 Choose and write the best answer, A, B or C.
1 Bears sometimes *swim* in rivers and lakes.
  A fly   B run   **C swim**
2 Snakes don't walk or run, but some snakes ____ .
  A swims   B swim   C hop
3 Bats ____ at night to look for food.
  A fly   B jump   C run
4 Meerkats ____ on four legs and sometimes stand on two legs.
  A run   B swim   C hop
5 Goats don't ____ .
  A fly   B jump   C walk
6 Dolphins ____ in some rivers in South America.
  A walk   B swim   C fly

5 Make sentences about the animals. Use a verb from Box 1 and a noun from Box 2.

Box 1

| ~~fly~~   eat   not like   sleep   swim   walk |

Box 2

| caves   desert   ~~forest~~   sea   spiders   water |

1 Parrots
   Parrots fly in the forest.
2 Sharks
   ____
3 Camels
   ____
4 Bats
   ____
5 Cats
   ____
6 Meerkats
   ____

LISTENING

1 🔊 3.1 Listen and choose the correct short answers.

1 Do black bears live in the national park?
  A Yes, they do.   B No, they don't.
2 Do brown bears live in Africa?
  A Yes, they do.   B No, they don't.
3 Do brown bears live in the mountains?
  A Yes, they do.   B No, they don't.
4 Do brown bears eat animals?
  A Yes, they do.   B No, they don't.
5 Are brown bears dangerous?
  A Yes, they are.   B No, they aren't.
6 Do brown bears sleep outside in the winter?
  A Yes, they do.   B No, they don't.

2 🔊 3.2 Listen again and complete the answers.
1 Q: Where is the national park?
  A: In *the USA* .
2 Q: When do brown bears usually look for food?
  A: In the ____ .
3 Q: Where do the bears in the national park sleep?
  A: Underground in the ____ .
4 Q: When do brown bears sleep?
  A: From ____ to April.
5 Q: When do mother bears have their babies?
  A: In ____ .
6 Q: What do baby bears do?
  A: They play a lot and learn to ____ .

GRAMMAR
Present simple: wh-questions

1 Match the questions (1–6) with the answers (a–f).

1 Where does it live? — c In the mountains.
2 What does it eat?
3 When does it sleep?
4 Has it got four legs?
5 Does it jump?
6 Is it a goat?

a Yes, it has.
b Yes, it is.
c In the mountains.
d Plants.
e Yes, it does.
f At night.

2 Complete the questions with these words.

> ~~Do~~ ×2   How   What   When   Where   Why

1 A _Do_ pandas live in groups?
  B No. They usually live alone.
2 A _____ do wild pandas live?
  B In China.
3 A _____ do they sleep?
  B At night.
4 A _____ do they eat?
  B Bamboo.
5 A _____ do they get their food?
  B They find it in the forest.
6 A _____ pandas swim?
  B Yes, they do.
7 A _____ don't pandas sleep in the cold months?
  B Because they eat every day.

3 Put the words in the correct order to make questions. Then choose the correct answer.

1 do/stand/on/two/legs/Why/meerkats
  Why do meerkats stand on two legs?
  To look for dangerous animals./To look for food.
2 bats/for/live/Do/30/years?
  _____
  Yes, they do./No, they don't.
3 live?/Where/kangaroos/do
  _____
  In Africa./In Australia.
4 What/do/meerkats/play?/game
  _____
  Volleyball./Hide-and-seek.
5 do/sloths/eat?/When
  _____
  At night./In the morning.
6 lions/food?/their/How/get/do
  _____
  They find plants./They hunt.

SPEAKING SKILLS

1 Read the questions about an animal. Choose the correct answer, A, B or C.

1 Where does it live?
  A Yes, it does.
  B In the jungle in Asia and Africa.
  C In September.
2 What does it eat?
  A Animals and birds.
  B Forests.
  C At night.
3 Has it got four legs?
  A No, it doesn't.
  B No, it isn't.
  C No, it hasn't.
4 Does it walk?
  A No, it isn't.
  B No, it hasn't.
  C No, it doesn't.
5 Does it swim?
  A Yes, sometimes.
  B No, it isn't.
  C In rivers.
6 Is it a snake? Is it a python?
  A Yes, it does.
  B Yes, it is.
  C Yes, it has.

26 GOLD EXPERIENCE

2 Read Sara and Irene's conversation about the photos. Choose the correct words.

Sara: Which is the odd one out?
Irene: I don't *know*/have/think.
Sara: I think it's a/*an*/the camel.
Irene: Why?
Sara: For/*Because*/Why it doesn't live in South America.
Irene: I don't think that's right/answer/wrong.
Sara: When/*What*/Who do you think?
Irene: I think the parrot is difference/same/*different* because it's small.
Sara: Yes, it is. Maybe that's right.
Irene: And because it *flies*/fly/flying and the other animals walk or run.

WRITING

1 Look at the table and complete the article about scorpions. Use one word in each space.

Scorpions	
Where do they live?	in all parts of the world – but not Antarctica
How big are they?	usually 6cm long
What do they eat?	Usually insects (e.g. beetles, spiders), some eat small animals
When do they feed?	at night
What do you know about them?	– some live in the desert (under the ground) – some eat one insect a year – dangerous to people – 4–8 babies, live on mother's back

Scorpions

Scorpions live all over the world, but they ¹ *don't* live in Antarctica. They live in cold and hot places. Some scorpions live in the ² _____ . They hide under the ground when it's hot. Scorpions are ³ _____ about 6cm long.

Scorpions go out at ⁴ _____ and look for food. They often eat insects such as beetles and ⁵ _____ , but they don't eat a lot of food. Some scorpions only eat one insect in a ⁶ _____ . Scorpions are sometimes dangerous to people.

Mother scorpions usually ⁷ _____ four to eight babies. They look after the babies when they are young. The babies live on their mother's back.

2 Choose the correct linking word.

1 Scorpions live in hot *and*/but/when cold countries.
2 They eat insects and/when/*but* they don't eat a lot.
3 Scorpions hide under the ground *when*/and/but it's hot.
4 Scorpions live in lots of places and/*but*/when they don't live in Antarctica.
5 Mother scorpions look after their babies and/but/*when* they're young.
6 Scorpions go out at night but/when/*and* look for food.

3 Use the information to write about cheetahs. Put the most important information first and use the words *and*, *but* and *when* to link your ideas.

Cheetahs	
Where do they live?	Africa and the Middle East
What colour are they?	Brown with black spots and white on the end of tail
How fast are they?	Can run at about 120 km/hour to hunt. 0–100 km/hour in 5 seconds
What do they eat?	Animals (e.g. gazelle, impala), sometimes big animals (e.g. zebra, wilderbeest)
When do they hunt?	During the day
Other interesting facts	Run fast to hunt but often don't catch any food

04 Around town

VOCABULARY
Places in town

1 Rearrange the letters to make places in town.

1. knba — *bank*
2. usuemm
3. rgdbie
4. glivael
5. hptosali
6. sbu atsiotn
7. wotn tneecr
8. trpsos enertc

2 Complete the table with these words.

cinema   market   park   ~~shop~~   square   supermarket   theatre

shop at the…	watch in the…	walk in the…
1) *shop*	4)	6)
2)	5)	7)
3)		

3 Look at the picture. Complete the sentences.

1. The swimming pool is next to the *park*.
2. The _____ is in front of the swimming pool.
3. The supermarket is between the _____ and the hospital.
4. The _____ is next to the hospital.
5. The park is near the _____.
6. The hospital is between the _____ and the café.

4 Read the clues and complete the words.

1. You jump on a bus here.
   b u s s t o p
2. You play volleyball here.
   s _ _ _ _ _ c _ _ _ _ _ _
3. It's a big place with shops or a market, but it isn't a city.
   t _ _ _
4. You walk your dog or play football here.
   p _ _ _
5. You watch films here.
   c _ _ _ _ _
6. There are many buses here.
   b _ _ s _ _ _ _ _ _

5 Read the text and choose the best answer, A, B or C.

Rome is a very interesting 1) *city*. There are lots of 2) _____ with important pictures. The River Tevere has got 31 3) _____. Next to the river there are restaurants and 4) _____. In the evening, buy a ticket and go to the 5) _____ to watch a play, or walk in a beautiful 6) _____. There are lots of 7) _____ on the streets or you can go by taxi. Why don't you buy a souvenir at one of the many 8) _____?

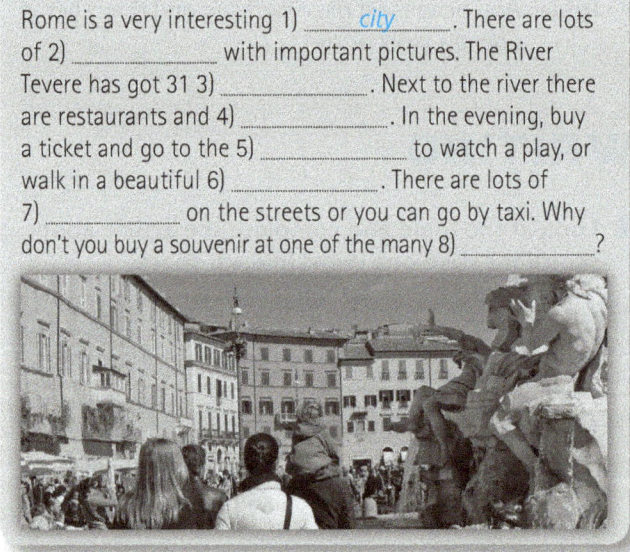

1. A village   B square   **C city**
2. A hospitals   B museums   C bridges
3. A cafés   B bridges   C theatres
4. A cafés   B hospitals   C sports centres
5. A bank   B supermarket   C theatre
6. A hospital   B square   C bank
7. A markets   B banks   C bus stops
8. A shops   B parks   C bridges

04 Around town

READING

1 Look at the map. Are the sentences (1–6) true (T) or false (F)?

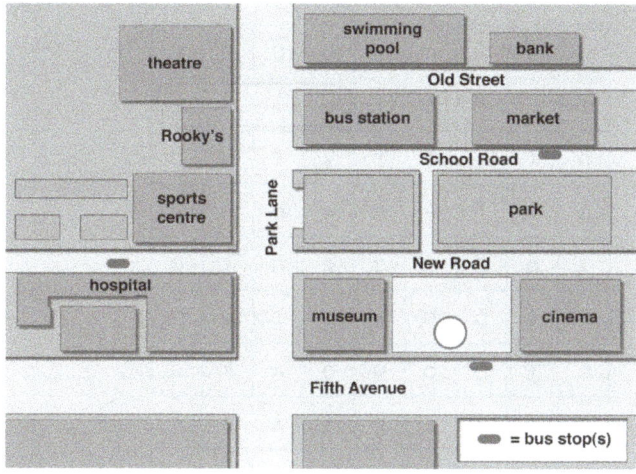

1 The bank is next to the sports centre. _F_
2 The bus station is near Fifth Avenue. ___
3 The cinema is between the bank and the theatre. ___
4 The hospital isn't near the park. ___
5 There's a bus stop in front of the hospital. ___
6 The museum is next to the cinema. ___

2 Read the instructions for a treasure hunt in a town. Put these sentences in the correct places.

> How much is a ticket to the town of Limerick?
> How much is a ticket for the play?
> Is it a café or a shop?
> ~~Can you find the name of this week's film?~~
> How many bus stops are there on New Road?

Morley treasure hunt!

Start in the square in the town centre. There's a cinema here.
1 _Can you find the name of this week's film?_
Walk across the square and go into the theatre.
2 ___
Leave the theatre on New Road.
3 ___
Walk to Park Lane and turn right. Look for Rooky's between the sports centre and the bank.
4 ___
There's a bus station near Rooky's.
5 ___

GRAMMAR
Imperatives

1 Match (1–6) with (a–f) to make imperatives.

1 Wait — b here!
2 Sit
3 Don't stand
4 Don't close
5 Please be
6 Don't

a the door!
b here!
c quiet.
d down, please.
e open your books!
f up.

2 Choose the correct place.

1 Don't run. It's dangerous.
   sports centre/<u>swimming pool</u>/park
2 Don't stand up.
   taxi/shop/city
3 Don't take photos.
   museum/village/bridge
4 Please be quiet.
   town centre/cinema/shop
5 Close the doors.
   school/market/bus stop
6 Don't play football.
   park/sports centre/museum
7 Wait here.
   supermarket/café/bus stop

3 Think about each place. Make positive or negative imperatives.

1 cinema (talk)   _Don't talk._
2 bus (close the doors)   ___
3 museum (touch the pictures) ___
4 school (listen)   ___
5 hospital (run)   ___
6 town centre (look at the map) ___

29

Subject and object pronouns

4 Complete the table.

Subject pronoun	Object pronoun
I	1) _me_
2) _____	you
he	3) _____
she	4) _____
5) _____	it
we	6) _____
7) _____	them

5 Choose the correct words.
1. We're in the cinema. Don't talk to *I/me*.
2. Look at the pictures in the museum, but don't touch *them/they*.
3. This is the bus stop. Wait here with *we/us*.
4. The theatre is open now. Please get Tom *his/him* ticket.
5. Do you want pictures of the town centre? You can buy *they/them* here.
6. I want a photo of us near the bridge. There's a woman…. ask *she/her*, please!

6 Complete the sentences with the correct pronoun.
1. I'm busy. Don't talk to _me_ .
2. Sergio is my best friend. I like _____ very much.
3. Don't touch those paintings. _____ are very old.
4. The café is near the bank. _____ is very good.
5. Marta isn't here. Text _____ .
6. Oh no! Our bus is at the bus stop. Bus! Please wait for _____ !
7. There's my aunt. _____ 's in front of the supermarket.

VOCABULARY
Vehicles

1 Find and write eight vehicles.

a	s	l	o	r	b	u	p	e
m	e	e	t	i	b	i	k	e
h	l	o	r	r	y	l	u	b
p	i	f	a	n	e	b	o	s
l	o	d	m	o	r	h	i	o
a	t	b	b	e	t	t	v	m
n	j	o	b	u	o	a	k	u
e	r	a	a	g	s	x	o	s
m	o	t	o	r	b	i	k	e

1. _bike_
2. _____
3. _____
4. _____
5. _____
6. _____
7. _____
8. _____

2 Write *air*, *road* or *sea*.
1. car — _road_
2. boat — _____
3. taxi — _____
4. van — _____
5. helicopter — _____
6. bike — _____
7. plane — _____

3 Choose the correct answer, A, B or C.
1. I've got a _bike_ and I always cycle to school.
   A car   **B bike**   C lorry
2. I love to fly. I like _____ .
   A planes   B trams   C vans
3. I travel by _____ every day. There's a stop near my house.
   A bike   B boat   C bus
4. I like to go by _____ on the road. I talk to the driver.
   A helicopter   B motorbike   C taxi
5. You can travel fast to different cities on a _____ . They are fantastic!
   A train   B bike   C tram
6. My parents take me to my swimming lessons in their _____ .
   A plane   B car   C train

04 Around town

4 Read about Pierre. Choose the best vehicle.

Pierre is from France. He travels in different vehicles. Which vehicle does he use to go …

1 from home to the village shop (200 metres)?
   lorry/*bike*/boat
2 from home to school (10 kilometres)?
   car/plane/helicopter
3 from home to the town centre (20 kilometres)?
   plane/bus/boat
4 from home to his grandparent's house (100 kilometres)?
   bike/tram/train
5 from the market in the town centre to the cinema (400 metres)
   tram/plane/helicopter
6 from Paris to London (350 kilometres)?
   plane/bike/taxi

5 Complete the text about Lisa's family with these words.

> ~~bike~~   bus   bus station   car   plane   train

" Every day I ride my 1) ___bike___ to the 2) _____. I go by 3) _____ to my school with my friends. My little brother goes by 4) _____ with my mum. My dad goes to work in the city on the 5) _____. He reads a book. My favourite vehicle is a 6) _____. We take one when we go on holiday. "

Lisa

LISTENING

1 🔊 4.1 Listen to a tour guide talking about Dublin. Choose the things he talks about.

1 cinemas ____	5 supermarkets _X_
2 parks _✓_	6 bridges ____
3 sports centres ____	7 shops ____
4 museums ____	8 cafés ____

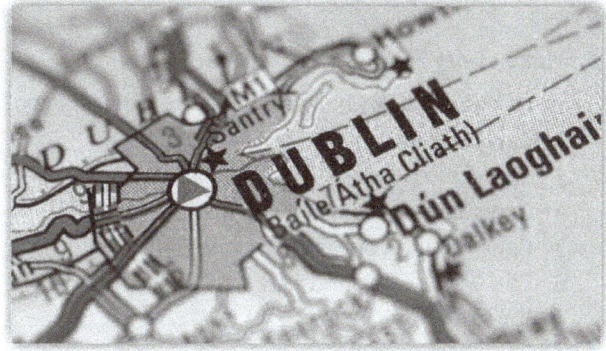

2 🔊 4.2 Listen to the tour guide again. Read the sentences and choose *can* or *can't*.

1 You *can/can't* go to the shops in Grafton Street.
2 You *can/can't* take photos in some of the museums.
3 You *can/can't* run around Phoenix Park.
4 You *can/can't* go on the water at Clara Lara Fun Park.
5 You *can/can't* have lunch at the fun park.
6 You *can/can't* look at Limerick from the O'Connell Bridge.
7 You *can/can't* go across the Halfpenny Bridge in a car.

GRAMMAR
Can for ability

1 Look at the table and make sentences. Use *can* or *can't*.

	swim	speak English	play volleyball	run 2km
Stefan	✗	✓	✓	✗
Mireia	✓	✗	✗	✓
Kirsten	✓	✓	✗	✗

1 Stefan *can't swim. He can speak English. He can play volleyball. He can't run 2km.*
2 Mireia _____
3 Kirsten _____

31

2 Match the questions (1–6) with the answers (a–f).

1 Can pandas swim?
2 Can a cat jump?
3 Can you speak English?
4 Can a dog talk?
5 Can your mum play volleyball?
6 Can Prince Charles speak French?

a Yes, I can.
b No, it can't.
c Yes, it can.
d Yes, they can.
e No, she can't.
f Yes, he can.

3 Make short answers for the questions.

1 Can you speak Chinese?   *No, I can't.*
2 Can penguins fly?
3 Can your dad sing?
4 Can your grandmother run fast?
5 Can you and your friends dance?
6 Can your best friend play the drums?
7 Can sharks swim?

Can for permission

4 Make sentences. Use *can* (✓) or *can't* (✗).

1 museum – take photos ✗
   You can't take photos.
2 cinema – talk ✗

3 park – play football ✓

4 swimming pool – run ✗

5 town centre – walk ✓

6 sports centre – play volleyball ✓

7 bank – sing ✗

5 Look at the photos and make questions.

1  go / the theatre
   Can I go to the theatre, please?

2  walk / my dog

3  sit / here

4  open / window

5  take / photos

6  jump / in the water

7  buy / ticket

8  cycle / here

04 Around town

SPEAKING SKILLS

1 Complete the conversation with these phrases.

> right at   ~~Excuse me~~   your left
> Brook Street   very much   Can you help me?
> straight on   Where's

A ¹ _Excuse me_ . Where's George Street, please?
² _____
B Yes, I can. You go ³ _____ and George Street is on ⁴ _____ .
A OK. Thanks. I want to go to the swimming pool there.
B The swimming pool is in ⁵ _____ , not George Street!
A Oh! ⁶ _____ Brook Street?
B You go straight on, then turn ⁷ _____ the bank. The swimming pool is on your right.
A Thanks ⁸ _____ .
B That's OK.

2 Look at the map. Start from 'You are here'. Choose the correct words to complete the directions.

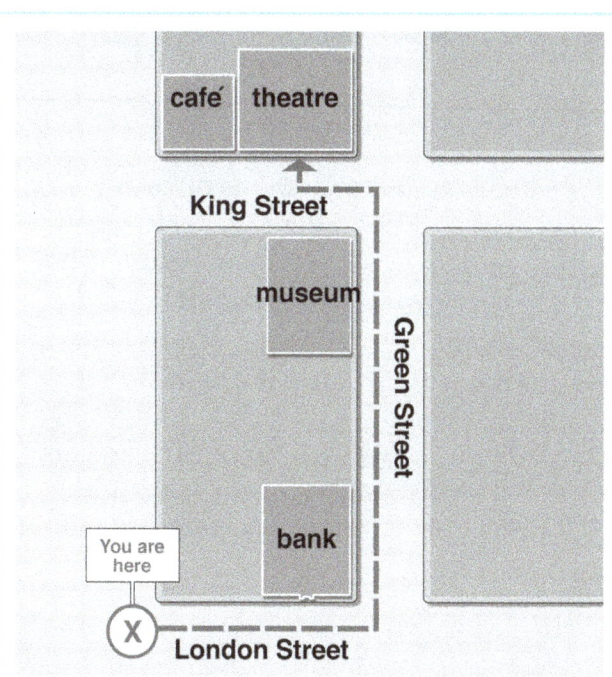

" Go ¹right/straight on, then turn ²right/left at the bank. Go straight on again and ³take/turn left again into ⁴King/London Street. The ⁵theatre/museum is ⁶in/on your right, ⁷next/between to the café. "

WRITING

1 Complete the email with these words. There are two words you do not need.

> at   Be   See   her   in   ~~me~~   to   we   with   you

View previous comments   Cancel   Share   Post

Can you meet ¹ _me_ and my sister at the café ² _____ Silver Street? It's ³ _____ birthday today! The café is near the bus stop. ⁴ _____ there ⁵ _____ 3 o'clock.
 We can have a coffee and some cake, then go swimming at the sports centre. Can you come ⁶ _____ the cinema ⁷ _____ us later?
See ⁸ _____ soon,
Olaf

Write a comment   Support

2 Match (1–8) with (a–h) to make sentences from a message.

1 Where — a cinema.
2 I'm in front of the   b later.
3 Can you come   c 15 minutes.
4 I'm sorry I'm   d at the bus station at 6?
5 Text me when   e late.
6 See you in   f to my party?
7 Can you meet me   g are you?
8 See you   h you get home.

3 Put the lines of this message in the correct order (1–6).

___ See you later.
___ Tania
___ Meet me at the swimming pool in Barrack Street.
___ Can you be there at 2.00?
_1_ Hi Mark,
___ Text me when you get this.

4 You want to meet a friend at the museum in town. Write a short message. Include the address, time and useful information. Remember to write a greeting and an ending.

Revision Units 3 – 4

VOCABULARY

1 Look at the photos. Complete the crossword puzzle.

2 Read the clues. Rearrange the letters to make animals and places.

1. They live under the ground in Africa.
   rkeetsma _____meerkats_____
2. It lives in the desert and it's big.
   mecal _____
3. It's usually in the town centre.
   uasqre _____
4. It lives in the mountains in Ecuador.
   maall _____
5. You usually go here by car to shop.
   mpuktserare _____

3 Choose the correct answer, A, B or C.

1. Sit down on the ___bus___ !
   A car   B lorry   **C** bus
2. I cycle to school. My _____ is green and white.
   A tram   B bike   C van
3. Don't _____ in the hospital, please.
   A walk   B run   C go
4. My grandmother often goes to the shops by _____ .
   A taxi   B helicopter   C fly
5. I like to fly to different countries on holiday. I love _____ !
   A bike   B planes   C motorbikes
6. _____ on a bus to go to the town centre.
   A Swim   B Run   C Jump
7. Helicopters usually _____ from city to city.
   A fly   B hop   C walk

4 Complete the postcard with these words.

> boats   ~~café~~   city   museum   River
> stops   trams   under

Hi Sam,
We're on holiday in Paris! Every morning we have breakfast at a little 1) __café__ near our hotel. Then we go by bus around the 2) _____ There are lots of bus 3) _____ . There aren't any 4) _____ here in Paris (not like Manchester!). In the afternoon we usually visit a 5) _____ . The 6) _____ Seine is beautiful. There are 7) _____ called bateaux mouches on the river. They go 8) _____ the bridges.
Love,
Emily

34 GOLD EXPERIENCE

Revision Units 3 – 4

GRAMMAR

1 Rewrite the sentences. Put the adverbs in the correct place.

1 Whales are big. (always)
   Whales are always big.

2 I walk to school. (often)

3 Bears swim. (sometimes)

4 Meerkats don't eat at night. (usually)

5 We go to the beach in December. (never)

6 My aunt is in her car. (always)

2 Choose the correct words.

1 *Who/What* do parrots eat?
2 Where *do/does* your dad play volleyball?
3 *When/Where* do scorpions live?
4 How *do/does* you get to the swimming pool?
5 When *do/does* the supermarket open?
6 *What/Why* do you always play computer games?
7 *When/Why* does this bus get to the town centre?

3 Put the words in the correct order.

1 take / photographs / I / can / please?
   Can I take photographs, please?

2 we / have / this afternoon? / party / Can / a

3 can't / on / play / I / football / Friday.

4 watch / please? / we / TV / Can

5 run / this / can't / in / You / museum.

6 can / People / swim / this / in / lake.

7 Felipe / to / run / the / village. / can

4 Look and make sentences.

1
   Don't talk.

2

3

4

5

6

5 Complete the conversation with one word in each space.

Boy: Excuse 1) *me*.
Girl: Yes.
Boy: Are you from this town?
Girl: Yes, I 2) _____.
Boy: 3) _____ do I get to the theatre?
Girl: It's here, next to the sports centre. Can 4) _____ see?
Boy: Oh, yes. It's not very near. Can I 5) _____ by bus?
Girl: Yes, 6) _____ can. The number 17. The bus stop is just there.
Boy: Where 7) _____ I buy a ticket?
Girl: You can buy 8) _____ on the bus.
Boy: Thanks for your help.
Girl: No problem.

05 Media magic

VOCABULARY
Jobs

1 Match the pictures with these jobs.

> dancer   film-maker   photographer
> police officer   taxi driver   ~~zoo-keeper~~

1

2

zoo-keeper

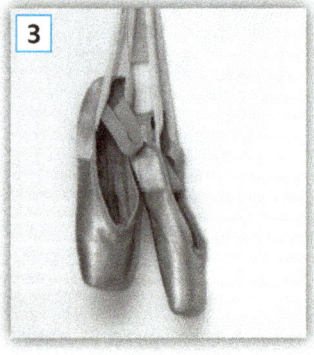
3

4

5

6

2 What's my job? Read the clues and complete the jobs.

1 I work in the town centre. I sometimes work at night. I'm a p _o_ _l_ _i_ _c_ _e_ o _f_ _f_ _i_ _c_ _e_ _r_.
2 I work in a theatre. I'm an a_____.
3 I work in a school. I'm a t_____.
4 I fly helicopters. I'm a p_____.
5 I play a sport. I'm a b_____ p_____.
6 I work in a zoo. I'm a z_____-k_____.

3 Match the sentences (1–6) with the jobs (a–f).

1 She can act.   a pilot
2 She can take good photographs.   b dancer
3 He likes planes.   c actor
4 He can dance.   d photographer
5 She can speak a different language. e zoo-keeper
6 He likes animals.   f Spanish teacher

4 Complete the blog about Luisa's family. Use one word in each space.

My family!

Cancel   Share   Post

The people in my family have got lots of different jobs. My dad loves animals but he isn't a zoo-keeper. He takes photographs of people's pets. He's a 1) _photographer_. My mum likes numbers. She's a maths 2) _____. My brother works at night. He drives a car. He's a taxi 3) _____. My uncle drives a car too, but it isn't a taxi. He's a police 4) _____. My aunt loves music. She's a 5) _____. My grandparents do the same job. My grandfather works in the theatre and my grandmother works in TV. They're 6) _____, but they're not famous.

Support

36 GOLD EXPERIENCE

05 Media magic

READING

1 Read the article. Choose the correct answer, A, B or C to complete the sentences.

Dancing queen

Anne Marie Stewart is 15. She's learning to be a dancer and she is in a dance competition in London next month. She talks to Teenagers Today about her life and we meet the people who are helping her.

'This is me. I'm jumping. I'm practising for the dance competition. My teacher is filming me with a video camera.'

'I'm not dancing in this photo. I'm watching the video with my teacher. We're checking my dance. It helps me to learn.'

'This is my mum. She's finishing my dress for the dance competition.'

'These are some of my friends from the dance school. They're dancing in the competition, too. They're good dancers. The competition is difficult, but I think we're all winners!'

1 Anne Marie is learning to ___dance___ .
  A dance **B** act **C** sing
2 The dance competition is in _____ .
  A France **B** Russia **C** Britain
3 Anne Marie's _____ films her when she's dancing.
  A father **B** mother **C** teacher
4 Anne Marie's _____ makes her dresses.
  A teacher **B** mother **C** father
5 Anne Marie's friends _____ in the competition.
  A aren't dancing **B** are dancing
  C are singing
6 Anne Marie thinks her friends are _____ dancers.
  A good **B** bad **C** not

2 Read the article. Complete the sentences with two words in each space.

1 Anne Marie is 15 ___years old___ .
2 Anne Marie _____ to dance.
3 Her teacher and her mother _____ her to be a dancer.
4 In the photo she's practising for a _____ .
5 Anne Marie is watching the video with _____ .
6 Anne Marie's _____ finishing her dress.
7 Anne Marie's friends _____ dancers.

GRAMMAR
Present continuous: be + verb + -ing

1 Complete the table with the correct present continuous forms.

	I	1) ___'m (am)___	
Positive	2) _____	's (is)	having lunch.
	We/You/They	3) _____	
Negative	I	'm (am) not	
	He/She/It	4) _____	5) _____ volleyball.
	6) _____	aren't (are not)	

Don't forget the spelling changes!
get – getting
take – 7) _____

2 Complete the sentences with the verbs in brackets. Use the present continuous.

1 I ___'m reading___ (read) a book.
2 My brother _____ (have) breakfast.
3 We _____ (not play) card games.
4 Look! The plane _____ (fly).
5 They _____ (swim) in the sea.
6 I _____ (make) lunch.
7 Agata and Kasia _____ (not watch) the film.
8 Xavier _____ (not cycle) to school.

3 Put the sentences about Bob's morning in the correct order. Number the lines (1–6).

It's 11 o'clock. Bob is having a cup of tea. ......
Bob is having a shower. ......
It's six o'clock. Bob is sleeping. __1__
Bob is getting dressed. ......
Bob is having lunch. ......
Bob is getting up. ......

4 Answer the questions. Use the words in brackets.

1 Q: Are you doing your homework?
  A: No. __I'm playing a game.__ (play a game)
2 Q: Is he flying to Barcelona?
  A: No. .... (take the train)
3 Q: Are they playing computer games?
  A: No. .... (watch TV)
4 Q: Are you going to the shops?
  A: No. .... (meet my friends)
5 Q: Is that kangaroo jumping?
  A: No. .... (hop)
6 Q: Are you playing the piano?
  A: No. .... (have a singing lesson)

5 Read the email and choose the correct word.

Subject: **Film-making workshop**

Hi Mum and Dad,
It's day three of my film-making workshop and I 1) *have/ 'm having* fun! Today I 2) *make/ 'm making* a film with my friends. I 3) *write/ 'm writing* this email because our teacher 4) *uses/ is using* the camera. She's an actor. She usually 5) *works/ 's working* in films and she sometimes 6) *makes/ 's making* films, too. I 7) *learn/ 'm learning* a lot. We 8) *'re having lunch/ have lunch* at the moment – the food here is great!
Love Sam

VOCABULARY
The weather

1 Match the symbols with these words.

cloudy   ~~cold~~   rainy   snowy   sunny   windy

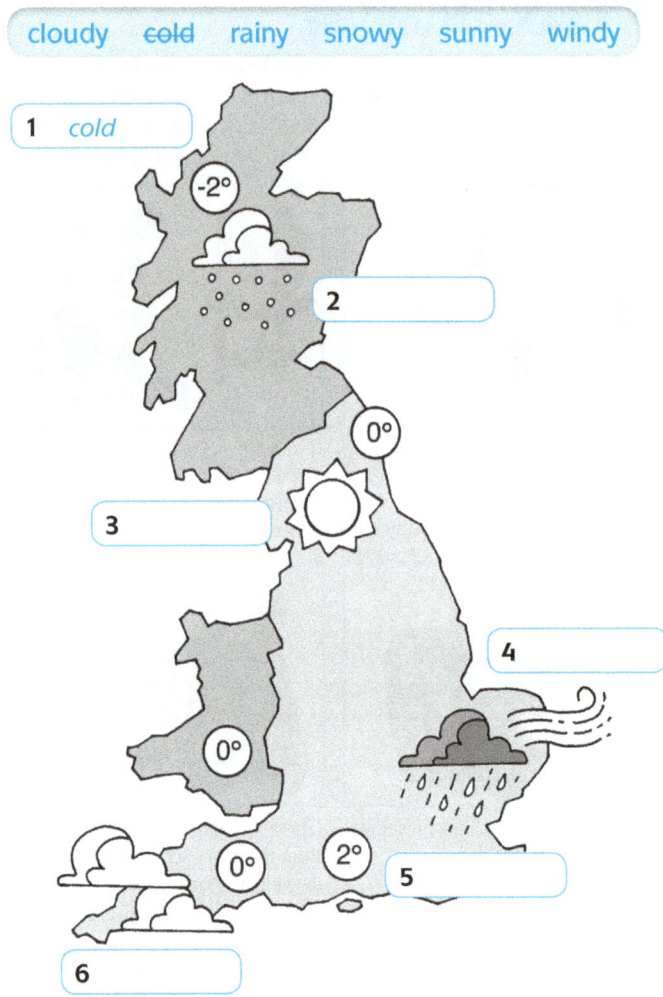

1 cold
2 ......
3 ......
4 ......
5 ......
6 ......

2 Find and write six weather words.

f	w	a	r	m	s	m
o	a	i	a	r	n	s
s	n	o	n	w	o	e
n	c	h	o	d	w	h
o	f	o	g	g	y	o
y	g	t	o	g	a	p
e	w	a	r	l	y	l

1 __windy__
2 ......
3 ......
4 ......
5 ......
6 ......

3 Complete the sentences.

1 Madrid, Spain   2 London, England

3 Ankara, Turkey   4 Warsaw, Poland

1 In Madrid it's ___hot___ and _____ .
2 In London it's _____ and _____ .
3 In Ankara it's _____ and _____ .
4 In Warsaw it's _____ and _____ .

4 Rearrange the letters to make seasons.

1 prinsg   ___spring___
2 reumms   _____
3 ntuaum   _____
4 reinwt   _____

5 Look at the table and complete the sentences.

Seasons in Britain

March	June	September	December
April	July	October	January
May	August	November	February

1 In Britain, July is in the ___summer___ .
2 September is in the _____ .
3 January is in the _____ .
4 August is in the _____ .
5 March is in the _____ .
6 February is in the _____ .

LISTENING

1 🔊 **5.1 Listen to Luigi talking about the Venice carnival. Are the sentences true (T) or false (F)?**

1 Day 1: The boys are making a film. __T__
2 Day 2: The boys are talking to a girl from Australia. ____
3 Day 3: They are watching a competition. ____
4 Day 4: The people are having singing lessons. ____
5 Day 5: The weather is cloudy. ____
6 Day 6: The boys are watching the boats. ____
7 Day 7: It's Saturday and they are listening to a music show. ____

2 🔊 **5.2 Listen to Luigi again. Choose the correct answer.**

1 On the first day of the carnival it's *cold/hot* and sunny.
2 Jimena is from *Argentina/Algeria*.
3 The competition is at eleven o'clock and *two/three* o'clock.
4 People are having dinner and *listening to music/dancing* at the Palazzo Ridotto.
5 The street theatre show starts at *nine/five* o'clock.
6 The theatre shows are in Italian, English and *German/French*.
7 The seventh day of the carnival is *Monday/Sunday*.

GRAMMAR
Present continuous questions

1 Match the questions (1–6) with the answers (a–f).

1 Is she helping her grandfather?
2 Are you all listening to me?
3 Is he enjoying the party?
4 Are the cats sleeping?
5 Are they acting in your film?
6 Are you talking to your parents, Emmanuel?

a Yes, we are.
b Yes, he is.
c Yes, I am. About the weekend.
d Yes, they are. And they're dancing, too.
e Yes, they are. They're over there.
f Yes, she is.

2 Make positive (+) or negative (−) short answers.

1 Is your brother shouting? (−)   *No, he isn't.*
2 Amelia, are you having a shower? (−) ....
3 Are your parents meeting their friends? (+) ....
4 Is she reading a good book? (+) ....
5 Are we watching a film? (+) ....
6 Is the film starting now? (−) ....

3 Make questions.

1 you / enjoy / that book
   Are you enjoying that book?
2 she / have / a guitar lesson
3 they / get up
4 he / play / volleyball
5 they / take / photos
6 you / film / this

Present continuous: wh- questions

4 Choose the correct answer, A, B or C.

1 *What* are you doing?
   A Why   **(B) What**   C Where
2 .... is the show finishing?
   A What   B Who   C When
3 .... are you taking photos?
   A Why   B Who   C What
4 .... are we having dinner?
   A What   B Who   C Where
5 .... is making breakfast?
   A When   B Who   C Where
6 .... is he watching on TV?
   A What   B Why   C What time

5 Complete the questions with the correct wh- words.

1 *Why* are you jumping? Are you cold?
2 .... are you learning to dance? Is it in the town centre?
3 .... is filming the show?
4 .... are you having breakfast at 2 o'clock in the afternoon?
5 .... is he checking – the lights?
6 .... is acting at the moment? Is it Sam or Leo?

6 Bartek is at a music festival. Read and complete the telephone conversations. Complete each space with two or three words.

Bartek: Hello?
Henryk: Hi, Bartek. It's Henryk. How are you?
1) *Are you enjoying* the music festival?
Bartek: Yes. I'm enjoying it a lot. I love camping, too.
Henryk: 2) .... doing now?
Bartek: I'm walking to the bus stop.
Henryk: 3) .... going to a bus stop?
Bartek: Because the camping isn't next to the arena. Oh … Here's the bus …
Henryk: Bartek?
Bartek: Yes? Is that you, Henryk?
Henryk Yes. Are you at the arena now?
4) .... watching?
Bartek: I'm watching Frozen Bird. They're really good.
Henryk: Wow! 5) .... they playing?
Bartek: They're playing *Walk Away*. It's my favourite song! Listen!
Henryk: 6) .... the piano?
Bartek: It's Radek. And Lula's singing.

05 Media magic

SPEAKING SKILLS

1 Look at the photo. Put the lines of the conversation in the correct order (1–6).

Katja: The zoo-keeper is talking about the penguins. The children are feeding them.

Katja: He's saying, 'Don't eat the fish!' ......

Thomas: Who are the people in the photo? __1__

Thomas: Yes, and I think the children are visiting the zoo. ......

Thomas: Yes, the children are giving them fish. What is the zookeeper saying? ......

Katja: I think that man is a zoo-keeper. ......

2 Complete the conversation with these words and phrases. There are two words or phrases you do not need.

> is making   are visiting   is taking   ~~Who~~
> is saying   think   What   visit

Karla: ¹ _Who_ are the people in that photo?

Richard: I ² .... it's a family. A mother, father and two children.

Karla: Yes, and I think they ³ .... Rome.

Richard: The father ⁴ .... a photo. The children aren't watching him.

Karla: Yes, the children are looking away. ⁵ .... is the father saying?

Richard: He ⁶ .... , 'Look at me and say "cheese"'!

WRITING

1 Match the instructions from an application form (1–7) with the information about Emma (a–g).

1 first name: a Brookes
2 last name: b 078322941165
3 age: c 13
4 address: d Emma
5 postcode: e 35 Nightingale Street, Camberwick
6 phone: f emmab@zoogle.com
7 email: g CW5 8YP

2 Read the email and complete the application form for Louis.

Dear Sir/Madam,

I'm Louis Rabier and I'm 14. My address is:
21 Greenway Road
London E12 6VB.

My mobile phone number is 079347551.

My favourite subjects at school are English and art. I want to be an actor when I finish school. I love acting and I'm doing a show at my school.

I want to do the acting class at your Theatre School. I've got singing lessons and football on Saturday, but I can come to the class on Friday after school.

Please send me the application form.
My email address is louistheactor@rmt.com.

Many thanks,
Louis

Theodora's Theatre School Application Form
Please write your name in BLOCK CAPITALS.

First name:	¹ _LOUIS_
Last name:	² ....
Address:	³ ....
Mobile number:	⁴ ....
Email:	⁵ ....
Age:	⁶ ....
Free-time activities:	I like acting, ⁷ .... and playing ⁸ ....

3 You want to go to a sports academy. Write some notes about you for an application form. Complete the application form. Include the following information.

Family name, First name, Address, Postcode, Telephone number, School, Age (years), Free time activities (no more than 20 words)

06 Fantastic food

VOCABULARY
Food and drink

1 Find and write eight food words in the word square.

r	c	a	r	r	a	b	r	a	i
m	i	p	s	a	l	e	s	e	d
l	s	c	h	e	e	s	e	g	e
k	c	i	e	e	s	h	g	e	a
m	a	f	o	r	a	n	g	e	l
z	r	u	m	i	l	a	t	r	m
o	r	i	b	e	a	n	s	o	i
i	o	t	y	o	d	u	w	j	l
e	t	o	r	d	e	a	t	s	k

1 _rice_
2 ....
3 ....
4 ....
5 ....
6 ....
7 ....
8 ....

2 Complete the food words.

1 s _a l a d_
2 c ....
3 b ....
4 c ....
5 f ....
6 y ....
   d ....

3 Complete the table with these food words.

~~banana~~   bread   chicken   egg   grapes
milk   orange   pasta

banana		

4 Choose the correct words.

1 Can I have a chicken _sandwich/pasta_, please?
2 I like _cheese/yoghurt_ drinks.
3 Try some pasta _salad/crisps_.
4 Do you like banana _cheese/milk_?
5 Enjoy your _orange/chicken_ salad.
6 I want an _vegetable/orange_ juice, please.

5 Choose the correct answer, A, B or C.

1 Can I have some __egg__ sandwiches?
  (A) egg   B rice   C milk
2 .... are good for you.
  A Carrots   B Crisps   C Cheese
3 .... drinks are my favourite.
  A Pasta   B Bread   C Yoghurt
4 Do you like .... juice?
  A bean   B rice   C orange
5 I have different types of .... for my breakfast.
  A pasta   B fruit   C carrot
6 Try some .... crisps.
  A grape   B milk   C chicken

READING

1 Read Emma's blog. Choose true (T) or false (F).

> Hi
>
> I'm Emma. I'm from Scotland and I'm doing a food science course.
>
> At the moment we're learning about healthy eating. We're looking at foods that give us energy. Beans, chicken and eggs are all good 'energy foods'. That's great because chicken with bean salad is my favourite meal! I also like eating nuts and seeds. They give me lots of energy.
>
> I make my lunch and take it to school, but some students have a hot lunch there. At school you can also buy fruit, milk and yoghurt drinks. There isn't any unhealthy food, like crisps! My friend says her favourite thing is the yoghurt drink.
>
> After this morning's class there's a test about fruit and vegetables. I've got an unhealthy snack to eat after the test – some chocolate!
>
> The food science course is for two years and it's hard work. Some of the students don't finish the course, but I love it!

1. Emma is from Scotland. _T_
2. Emma is doing food science. ___
3. Emma says that bread, cheese and milk give you energy. ___
4. Nuts and seeds are good for energy. ___
5. At school you can buy crisps. ___
6. Emma has got a test about energy foods today. ___
7. All of the students finish the food science course. ___

2 Read Emma's blog and choose the best answer to each question, A or B.

1. What does Emma like to eat?
   A eggs   (B) bean salad
2. Does Emma have a hot lunch at school?
   A Yes, she does.   B No, she doesn't
3. What can Emma buy for lunch at school?
   A healthy food   B unhealthy food
4. Who likes the yoghurt drink?
   A Emma   B Emma's friend
5. What food has Emma got?
   A chocolate   B fruit
6. How long does the food science course last?
   A two years   B a morning

06 Fantastic food

GRAMMAR
Countable and uncountable nouns (some/any)

1 Complete the table with these food words.

> banana   bread   carrot   chicken sandwich
> fruit   salad   rice   ~~yoghurt drink~~

countable	uncountable
yoghurt drink	

2 Choose the correct answer, A, B or C.

1. I need __some__ bread for my lunch.
   A a   (B) some   C any
2. Are there _____ eggs in the kitchen?
   A an   B any   C a
3. You need to eat _____ orange for your cold.
   A some   B a   C an
4. I want _____ chicken sandwich, please.
   A any   B some   C a
5. There aren't _____ bananas in the fruit salad.
   A any   B an   C a
6. He usually has _____ egg with his rice.
   A some   B an   C any

A lot (of)/much/many

3 Make questions. Use How much or How many.

1. oranges / you / have got
   How many oranges have you got?
2. rice / be / there
   _____
3. eggs / you / need
   _____
4. carrots / be / there
   _____
5. pasta / you / need
   _____
6. bread / be / there
   _____

43

4 Match the questions (1–6) with the answers (a–f).

1 How many apples are there?
2 Is there much water on the table?
3 How many sandwiches have you got?
4 How much milk have you got?
5 Are there a lot of eggs in the salad?
6 How much rice do you need?

a We haven't got much. Half a litre.
b There are six.
c We need a lot. Two kilos.
d No, there aren't.
e Yes, there's a lot. I'm sorry.
f I haven't got many. Two cheese and one chicken.

5 Complete the sentences with *any*, *some*, *much*, *many* or *a lot*.

1 I don't usually have ___any___ coffee with my breakfast. I don't like it.
2 There aren't _____ drinks on the menu, just cola, water and milk.
3 I always have _____ biscuits with hot milk in the morning.
4 How _____ snacks do I eat in a day? _____, I'm sorry to say!
5 My brother doesn't eat _____ fruit. He isn't very healthy.
6 There are _____ of types of pasta.

6 Complete the text with these words.

> a lot of   cheese   egg   ~~fruit~~
> not many   some

School dinners

The food at school is fantastic! In the morning we have a 'snack shop'. There are usually healthy snacks, some 1) ___fruit___, like bananas or grapes, and sandwiches. At lunchtime there are hot dinners, but 2) _____ students have the dinners because they have sandwiches from home. There is 3) _____ different food: rice, pasta with tomato sauce, bread, chicken and vegetables. Sometimes I have an 4) _____ with salad and lots of 5) _____. I often have fruit or 6) _____ orange juice. Delicious!

VOCABULARY
Health problems

1 Read the clues, then rearrange the letters to make words about health problems.

1 When you are too hot you have a ___temperature___. patteuemrre.
2 Orange juice is good for a _____. docl
3 I've got a _____. Keep away! oguch
4 I can't eat carrots. I've got _____. othchotae
5 Crisps are bad for my _____ _____. rseo httoar
6 When I eat eggs I get a _____. omscahtceha

2 Match the words with the photos.

> ~~cold~~   earache   headache   sore throat
> stomachache   toothache

1 cold

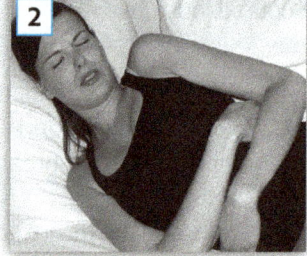

2 _____

3 _____

4 _____

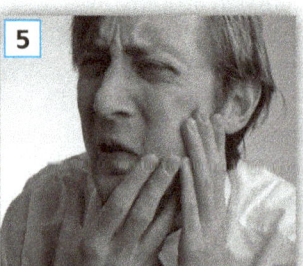

5 _____

6 _____

44 GOLD EXPERIENCE

Fantastic food

3 Choose the correct answer, A, B or C.

1 I've got a *temperature* of 39 degrees.
  A cold (B) temperature C cough
2 I can't eat. I've got a _____ .
  A stomachache B earache C cold
3 I can't talk. I've got a _____ .
  A stomachache B sore throat C temperature
4 I'm eating an orange because I've got a _____ .
  A toothache B stomachache C cold
5 Be quiet! I've got a _____ .
  A headache B sore throat C cough
6 I can't hear you. I've got _____ .
  A cold B earache C toothache

4 Complete the conversation.

Tara: Hi, Ali. Are you OK?
Ali: No, I feel really 1) h *ot* _____ .
Tara: Have you got a 2) t _____ ?
Ali: I don't know. But I've got a 3) s _____ t _____ , too.
Tara: Oh dear. Why don't you go to the doctor's?
Ali: No, I think it's just a 4) c _____ .

5 Read the doctor's advice and make sentences. Use these words and *I've got*.

> cold   earache   headache   sore throat
> stomachache   ~~temperature~~

1 Stay indoors. Go to bed.
2 Don't listen to your music player.
3 Don't talk too much.
4 Always wash your hands after you clean your nose.
5 Don't eat.
6 Take some medicine. Stay in a quiet place.

1 *I've got a temperature.*
2 _____
3 _____
4 _____
5 _____
6 _____

LISTENING

1 🔊 6.1 Listen to two friends talking about a sports competition. Match (1–6) with (a–f) to make sentences.

1 Mrs Fernandez — a is watching the running.
2 Maribel   b has got a stomachache.
3 Mr Valdez   c has got a sore throat.
4 Megan   d has got a bad cold.
5 Ben   e is taking photographs.
6 Mr Ruano   f is in the volleyball competition.

2 🔊 6.2 Listen again. Choose the correct phrase.

1 Jorge and Miguel *don't have to/have to* do a lot of training.
2 Angela *has to/doesn't have to* run in the competition.
3 Megan *can/can't* run today.
4 Ben *can/can't* swim in the competition this afternoon.
5 Maribel *has to/doesn't have to* eat special food.
6 Maribel *can't/can* eat crisps and sweets.
7 Maribel *doesn't have to/has to* practise volleyball every day.
8 Angela and Juan *don't have to/have to* move to watch the volleyball.

GRAMMAR
Have to/Don't have to

1 Choose the correct words.
1 I *has to/have to* be at school at eight o'clock.
2 My brother *has to/have to* do a lot of homework.
3 We *has to/have to* wash our hands before we eat.
4 Tomas *has to/have to* eat lots of fruit to be healthy.
5 Students *has to/have to* go home at three o'clock.
6 My sister *has to/have to* practise the guitar a lot.

2 Look at the photos and make sentences.

1 be quiet
   You have to be quiet.

2 walk

3 wash hands

4 be school 8 o'clock

3 Make negative sentences.
1 She has to help at home.
   She doesn't have to help at home.
2 I have to cook dinner tonight.

3 He has to get up at 7 o'clock at the weekend.

4 We have to have lunch early today.

4 Complete the paragraph with the verbs and the correct form of *have to* or *don't have to*.

I play in my school's football team. We 1) *have to practise* (practise) a lot, but we 2) _____ (play) football matches every day. Sometimes we just run and jump. When there's a match on a Saturday, I 3) _____ (get up) early. I go to school by car with my mum to meet my friends. Then we 4) _____ (go) to a different town by bus. My mum 5) _____ (watch). She doesn't like football anyway. When we play we 6) _____ (run) a lot and we 7) _____ (drink) lots of water.

5 Match the questions (1–7) with the answers (a–g).
1 Do you have to do a lot of homework?
2 Does your dad have to work at night?
3 Do you have to take medicine for a cold?
4 Does your sister have to cook dinner tomorrow?
5 Do they have to be quiet in the museum?
6 Do I have to go to bed at nine o'clock?
7 Do we have to make the cake for tomorrow?

a No, you don't. You can drink orange juice.
b No, he doesn't.
c Yes, she does.
d Yes, you do.
e Yes, I do. Two hours a day.
f Yes, they do.
g No, we don't. It's for Thursday.

6 Make questions. Use *have to*.
1 you / get up at seven o'clock
   Do you have to get up at seven o'clock?
2 your brother / go to the shops today

3 your friends / eat lunch at school

4 your mum / go to work / on Saturday

5 we / eat fruit for breakfast

6 I / take the dog for a walk

06 Fantastic food

SPEAKING SKILLS

1 Read the sentences in a restaurant. Does the waiter (W) or the customer (C) say the sentences?

1 No, sorry. We haven't got any fish. _W_
2 I'd like a smoothie, please. ____
3 Can I have some water? ____
4 Would you like a drink? ____
5 Yes, please. ____
6 No, thanks. ____
7 What would you like? ____
8 Would you like some food? ____
9 Er … Let me think. A chicken sandwich, please. ____

2 Choose the correct words to complete the conversation at a café.

Waitress: Hello! ¹_Would_/_Do_ you like a drink?
Girl: Yes. Can I have ²_some_/_a_ yoghurt drink, please?
Waitress: OK. Would you like ³_some_/_a_ food?
Girl: Yes. Just ⁴_some_/_a_ minute. … I'd like a sandwich. What sandwiches ⁵_do_/_would_ you have?
Waitress: We have chicken salad or cheese sandwiches.
Girl: That's not ⁶_many_/_much_. Let me think. … I'd like cheese, please.
Waitress: Would you like ⁷_some_/_a_ crisps with that?
Girl: Er, no, thanks.

WRITING

1 Put the words in the correct order to make sentences.

1 Bread is in lots of food 'pairs'.
   eat / example, / people / For / jam. / bread / and
   For example, people eat bread and jam.

2 Some 'pairs' of food are strange.
   is / with / Tea / milk / UK. / popular / in / the
   ____

3 You can eat chips with vinegar.
   I / tomato / chips / ketchup. / like / with
   ____

4 Some food pairs are famous.
   and / eat / example, / British / fish / people / chips. / For
   ____

5 Have you got a favourite food?
   pairs / food / Which / of / do / like? / you
   ____

2 Complete the article with one word in each space.

What food is healthy?

It's good to eat lots of fruit. It's healthy and it has vitamins. It helps when you are ill. ¹ _For_ example, when I've got ² ____ cold, I eat oranges.

Do you like salads? I love them. They're delicious and they're good ³ ____ you too, ⁴ ____ course! I always put in beans and carrots.

What's your favourite snack? I really like chocolate, but I don't often eat ⁵ ____. My favourite healthy snack is a banana. My dad says I'm strange ⁶ ____ I like banana sandwiches. I also eat apples ⁷ ____ grapes and other fresh fruit.

3 Complete the plan for an article with these words. There are two words you do not need.

cold   coffee   likes   ~~hot~~   drink
orange   My   very   not

Different ideas all over the world about drinks:
Britain - ¹ _hot_ drinks (e.g. tea and hot chocolate).
Italy - lots of ² ____ (e.g. espresso, cappuccino).
Many people ³ ____ cola - ⁴ ____ healthy
⁵ ____ favourite drink - ⁶ ____ juice, delicious!

4 Write a short article using the plan. Remember to use _of course_ and _for example_.

Revision Units 5 - 6

VOCABULARY

1 Choose the correct words.

1 Don't play football today. You've got a *temperature/toothache* and it's cold outside.
2 I sometimes don't work when it's foggy. I'm a *pilot/teacher*.
3 Do you like animals? You can be a *pet/zoo-keeper*.
4 My sister doesn't eat *chicken/juice*.
5 I can't eat that cheese. I've got a *toothache/cold*.
6 I don't want to watch TV. I've got a *stomachache/headache*.
7 *Carrots/Oranges* are a type of vegetable.

2 Read the clues and complete the words.

1 I want to be a d _a_ _n_ _c_ _e_ _r_. I have to practise a lot.
2 James Cameron is a famous film-m _____ _____ _____ from the USA.
3 Juan Carlos Navarro is a basketball p _____ _____ _____ _____ from Spain.
4 I'm a good p _____ _____ _____ _____ _____ _____ _____. I'm taking photos for a competition.
5 Our teacher can't talk today. She's got a sore t _____ _____ _____ _____ _____.
6 I've got a headache and a cough. I think I've got a c _____ _____ _____.
7 Eat some yoghurt. It's good for your s _____ _____ _____ _____ _____ ache.
8 His t _____ _____ _____ _____ _____ _____ _____ _____ _____ is 37 degrees. I think he's OK.

3 Complete the blog with these words.

> driver   officer   ~~rainy~~   snowy
> spring   warm

My mum works in our town. She has to walk a lot. She often has to work when it's 1) _rainy_, and in the winter, when it's cold and 2) _____. But she likes her job. She helps people. She's a police 3) _____. My dad is always in his car. He's a taxi 4) _____ in the city. He likes to work in the 5) _____, when the weather is 6) _____, but not too hot.

4 Look at the photos. Complete the crossword puzzle.

5 Look at the table and complete the sentences.

1 In Buenos Aires in the _summer_ it's hot and sunny.
2 In London in the _____ it's usually windy.
3 The weather in London is often rainy and _____ in the spring.
4 In July in Buenos Aires it's sometimes _____.
5 _____ in London is from June to August.
6 In January in London it's snowy and _____.

	Buenos Aires, Argentina	London, England
Spring	September–November 22°	March–May 13°
Summer	December–February 29°	June–August 20°
Autumn	March–May 23°	September–November 10°
Winter	June–August 16°	December–February 7°

48 GOLD EXPERIENCE

Revision Units 5–6

GRAMMAR

1 Complete the sentences with the verbs in brackets. Use the present continuous.

1 We __'re writing__ (write) a book about an actor.
2 Be quiet, please! I _____ (do) my homework.
3 Dad _____ (make) breakfast this morning.
4 Justine and Nathalie aren't here. They _____ (play) volleyball.
5 Why are you texting your sister? She _____ (sit) over there!
6 _____ you _____ (go) to the shops?
7 _____ the party _____ (finish) now?
8 _____ the boys _____ (have) a singing lesson at the moment?

2 Put the words in the correct order.

1 playing / drums? / Who / the / is
   __Who is playing the drums?__
2 they / here? / What / are / doing
3 on / She's / to / the / talking / phone. / her / friend
4 What / watching / now? / you / are
5 do / You / have / homework. / to / your
6 have / to / swimming / we / Do / have / lessons?
7 Pietro / make / Does / have / his / lunch? / to
8 We / get / up / have / at / to / o'clock. / six

3 Look at the picture and make sentences. Use *There's/There are* or *There isn't/There aren't*.

1 salad — __There's some salad.__
2 egg
3 bread
4 oranges
5 bananas
6 crisps
7 pasta

4 Read the conversation. Choose the correct answer, A, B or C.

Maria: We 1) __'re__ making some sandwiches for the party. How 2) _____ do we have 3) _____ make?
Oscar: About 20.
Maria: That's 4) _____ of sandwiches.
Oscar: I know, but the party is at 12 o'clock. My friends usually 5) _____ a lot at lunchtime.
Maria: OK. Can you get 6) _____ cheese for the sandwiches at the supermarket?
Oscar: Yes. How 7) _____?
Maria: 500 grams.
Oscar: Do I have to get 8) _____ drinks?
Maria: No, that's OK. We've got a lot of cola.

1	**A** 're	B	's	C	'm
2	**A** much	B	many	C	some
3	**A** we	B	to	C	that
4	**A** a lot	B	many	C	much
5	**A** 're eating	B	eats	C	eat
6	**A** a lot	B	much	C	some
7	**A** much	B	many	C	do
8	**A** a	B	any	C	a lot

5 Complete the sentences with *has to* or *have to* in the positive or negative form.

1 Beatríz __has to__ take some medicine. She's got a temperature.
2 Teachers _____ work at night.
3 Football players _____ run a lot.
4 I _____ go to school in July or August. It's the holidays.
5 My brother _____ do homework. He's only five.
6 She can't sing. She _____ have some lessons!

Life in the past

VOCABULARY
Dates

1 Complete the table.

Cardinal number (How many)	Ordinal number (Order)
one	first
1) _two_	second
three	2) ....
four	3) ....
4)	fifth
six	5) ....
6)	seventh
eight	7) ....
nine	8) ....
ten	tenth

2 Put the dates in the order they happen.

> the twenty-fourth of May   ~~the third of May~~
> the twentieth of May   the twenty-ninth of May
> the fifteenth of May   the thirty-first of May
> the twelfth of May   the twenty-fifth of May

1 the third of May
2 ....
3 ....
4 ....
5 ....
6 ....
7 ....
8 ....

3 Match the numbers with the way we say the dates.

1 the first of August
2 ....
3 ....
4 ....
5 ....
6 ....
7 ....

> the twenty-first of August
> the sixth of August   the sixteenth of August
> ~~the first of August~~   the thirtieth of August
> the thirteenth of August
> the twenty-sixth of August

4 Read and complete the table.

1 In the USA, Independence Day is on the fourth of July.
2 In Poland, Teacher's Day is on the fourteenth of October.
3 In Argentina, the twentieth of June is National Flag Day.
4 In the UK it is Bonfire Night on the fifth of November.
5 The twenty-third of April is special in Turkey. It's Children's Day.
6 Australia Day is on the twenty-sixth of January.

Country	Date	Holiday
USA	4 July	Independence Day
1) _Poland_	2)	Teacher's Day
Argentina	3)	4) ....
5)	5 November	6) ....
Turkey	7)	Children's Day
Australia	8)	Australia Day

5 Match the way we say the years (1–8) with the numbers (a–h).

1 nineteen twenty — g 1920
2 seventeen hundred
3 seventeen fifty-five
4 sixteen fifty-five
5 twenty nineteen
6 nineteen oh two
7 two thousand and five
8 twenty fifty

a 2019
b 2050
c 1902
d 2005
e 1655
f 1700
g 1920
h 1755

50 GOLD EXPERIENCE

READING

1 Read what Jenny says about her visit to a school museum. Choose true (T) or false (F).

I'm on holiday in a village in England this week. Today I'm at a school museum, where you can travel back in time to the 1900s! The village here is small and the school is opposite a field with animals. It's very different from my school. There's a big, special room called a school room, not a classroom. And the toilets are outside the school!

Life in the village in the past was very different from today. There weren't any computer games – children played with their friends outside or they played card games with their families. The children were busy with their work for their families when they weren't at school. There was washing and cleaning to do. And they were busy looking after the horses and cows at home. There wasn't much free time for music and TV. I like the school museum, but I like life today too!

Jenny

1 The village is big. _F_
2 The school is in a field with animals. ____
3 There is a room for children called a classroom. ____
4 There aren't any toilets inside the school. ____
5 There weren't any computer games. ____
6 There was a cow and a horse at the school. ____

2 Read what Jenny says about her visit to a school museum. Write short answers.

1 Was Jenny on holiday in Spain?
   No, she wasn't.
2 Was the school museum the same as Jenny's school?
   ____
3 Were there any toilets at the school?
   ____
4 Did children in the 1900s have lots of free time?
   ____
5 Did children help to clean the house in the 1900s?
   ____
6 Did Jenny like the museum?
   ____

GRAMMAR
Past simple: be

1 Choose the correct words.
1 There *was*/were one room in a Frontier House.
2 In 1883 there *are/were* card games and guitars, not TVs.
3 There *is/was* a lot of work to do today. Can you help me?
4 There *are/were* horses and a cow for each family in a Frontier House.
5 There *are/were* lots of cars in cities now.
6 Every day *was/were* the same in 1883.

2 Change these sentences into the past simple.
1 There isn't a supermarket in our village.
   There wasn't a supermarket in our village.
2 There aren't any eggs.
   ____
3 The food isn't very good at that restaurant.
   ____
4 Cristina isn't busy.
   ____
5 Frontier houses aren't very big.
   ____
6 My mum and dad aren't happy with me.
   ____

3 Complete the blog. Use the correct form of *be* in the past simple.

My family!

Cancel   Share   Post

On Friday, my history class 1) _was_ at a museum. It 2) ____ in the town centre and there 3) ____ lots of photographs of our town in the past. In 1910 there 4) ____ many cars in the town. There 5) ____ horses and trams. The high street 6) ____ busy but the shops 7) ____ small. There 8) ____ any big supermarkets.

Support

4 Match the questions (1–6) with the answers (a–f).

1 Were your grandparents happy to see you?
2 Was the town busy on Saturday morning?
3 Was your sister at the party?
4 Were you and your brother in bed at 10 o'clock?
5 Was Daniel in class yesterday?
6 Was I good in the show?

a Yes, we were.
b Yes, they were.
c Yes, he was.
d Yes, you were.
e Yes, she was.
f Yes, it was.

5 Make negative short answers.

1 Was your uncle at the sports centre?
   No, he wasn't.
2 Were there any oranges in the cupboard?
3 Was it foggy yesterday?
4 Were you at home on Sunday, Amelia?
5 Were the chicken sandwiches OK?
6 Was your mum on the train yesterday afternoon?

6 Complete the conversation. Use the past simple of *be* and short answers.

1 Alejandro: *Were* there many cafés in town?
   Granddad: No, *there weren't*.
2 Alejandro: _____ there a cinema?
   Granddad: Yes, _____.
3 Alejandro: _____ you a pilot?
   Granddad: Yes, _____.
4 Alejandro: _____ Mum a good student?
   Granddad: No, _____.
5 Alejandro: _____ Grandma a good dancer?
   Granddad: Yes, _____.
6 Alejandro: _____ the shops different in town?
   Granddad: Yes, _____.
7 Alejandro: _____ there many houses in our street?
   Granddad: No, _____.

VOCABULARY
Common verbs

1 Read the clues. Complete the crossword puzzle.

Down
1 After I play football, I c *hange* my clothes.
2 Do you often t_____ your friends?
5 Does Barbara usually v_____ her grandmother on Saturday?
6 I live near my school, so I w_____ there every morning with my dad.

Across
3 We s_____ with our cousins on holiday.
4 You can t_____ from London to Paris by train, boat or plane.
7 When does the bus a_____ in the town centre?
8 We _____ our lunch at 1 o'clock.

Crossword: 1 Down: C H A N G E

2 Match (1–7) with (a–g) to make sentences.

1 Ethan travels to his grandfather's house   *g*
2 He usually arrives
3 They talk about
4 Ethan helps his granddad in
5 They tidy
6 Then they change
7 After dinner, they walk

a their clothes.
b the garage together.
c in the morning.
d football.
e in the woods with the dog.
f the garden.
g by car.

07 Life in the past

3 Read and choose the best answer, A, B or C.

Cristina always 1) *visits* her cousins in the spring. They live near the beach. She 2) _____ for a week. She 3) _____ there by car with her mum and dad. They usually 4) _____ in the evening. Cristina and her cousins 5) _____ on the beach every day and they 6) _____ for hours.

1	A changes	B visits	C arrives
2	A arrives	B tidies	C stays
3	A talks	B walks	C travels
4	A arrive	B stay	C change
5	A wash	B walk	C tidy
6	A talk	B arrive	C help

4 Complete the blog with these verbs.

arrive   help   stay   text   walk   ~~wash~~

My family!

Cancel   Share   Post

Saturday is my favourite day of the week. I usually get up at seven o'clock and I 1) *wash* my hair. I have breakfast and then I 2) _____ my dad at the market. We 3) _____ there because it's near my house. We 4) _____ at about half past eight and we 5) _____ all morning. After lunch I 6) _____ my friends and we go to the cinema or the sports centre. We have lots of fun.

LISTENING

1 🔊 7.1 Read about Havers Hall. Listen and choose the correct word or phrase.

Welcome to Havers Hall

The hall was a ¹*family home*/museum/theatre for 500 years.

See the old kitchen, the dining room and bedrooms. Go on the balcony and look at the ²*horses/cows/sheep* in the fields.

Meet friends and ³*have breakfast/have lunch/have dinner* in the café or visit the ⁴*garage/market/shop*.

Walk around our fantastic ⁵*rooms/gardens/forests*. They are opposite the house.

Children can also ⁶*play/feed the animals/stay in the gardens*.

And finally ... new in August! The travel back in time day! ⁷*Have a party/Make a film/Stay the night* in the hall ... Phone or email for more details.

2 🔊 7.2 Listen to the telephone message about Havers Hall. Complete the sentences with one word in each space.

1 For garden opening dates, press ___*two*___.
2 The hall is open from 5 April to _____ September.
3 The gardens are open from 1 _____ to 31 October.
4 School visits are on 3 May, _____ June and 8 September.
5 The travel back in time day this year is on 2 _____.
6 Thank you and enjoy your _____!

GRAMMAR
Past simple: regular verbs

1 Make the past simple form of these verbs.

1 talk _talked_
2 stop _____
3 arrive _____
4 tidy _____
5 change _____
6 travel _____
7 walk _____

2 Choose the correct answer, A, B or C.

1 The train _didn't_ arrive at 9.30.
  A wasn't B isn't **C didn't**
2 She _____ her parents after the party.
  A text B texted C did text
3 They _____ us to cook dinner.
  A didn't help B helps C not helped
4 We _____ a film last night, but it wasn't very good.
  A watched B was watching C watch
5 Michele _____ computer games last night.
  A wasn't playing B didn't play C play
6 We _____ the kitchen before my parents arrived.
  A cleaning B clean C cleaned

3 Correct the sentences. Use the past simple in the positive or negative form.

1 John Lennon played the drums.
  John Lennon didn't play the drums.
2 Christopher Columbus arrived in America in 1942.
  _____
3 Julius Caesar travelled by bus.
  _____
4 Michelangelo didn't visit Rome.
  _____
5 In 1750 people cleaned their teeth every day.
  _____
6 In 1920 most people didn't walk to school.
  _____

4 Complete the article with these verbs. Use the past simple in the positive or negative form.

~~arrive~~   change   help   play   talk   travel   wash   watch

Pop star!

Mason playing live

A pop star – but not to his mum and dad!
Mason is a famous pop star, but he lives with his parents. He 1) _arrived_ home from a concert yesterday evening. He travelled by train. He 2) _____ by helicopter, because he doesn't like flying. He always changes after a concert, so he 3) _____ his clothes and he 4) _____ his hair. He 5) _____ TV – there aren't any TVs in his parents' house. Mason 6) _____ to his parents about the concert. They talked about other things. He likes to cook, so he 7) _____ his parents to make dinner. He 8) _____ his guitar because he doesn't like to play it after a concert.

SPEAKING SKILLS

1 Complete the conversation with these words.

2011   week   September   ~~yesterday~~   Saturday   night

1 A I played cards _yesterday_. What about you?
  B I watched TV.
2 A We travelled by train to the football match on _____. What about you and your family?
  B We travelled by train, too.
3 A In the UK we started school in _____. What about in Italy?
  B We started in October.
4 A Did you visit the museum last _____?
  B Yes. It was fantastic!
5 A Did your brother listen to his MP3 player last _____?
  B No, he didn't. I listened to it!
6 A When did your teacher arrive at your school?
  B In _____.

54 GOLD EXPERIENCE

07 Life in the past

2 Put the questions and answers in the correct places to complete the conversation.

> Next question? Were they from France?
> What do you think? Is that right? I think I do.
> That isn't right. ~~Do you know the answers?~~

Ana: I'm having problems with this history homework. You know, the quiz about the Romans. ¹ *Do you know the answers?*

Maria: ² _____ I watched a programme about the Romans last week.

Ana: Great! Well, the first question. Where were the Romans from? ³ _____

Maria: No, the Romans were from Italy. ⁴ _____

Ana: OK, 2. How did the Romans travel? I think the Romans travelled in cars. ⁵ _____

Maria: No. ⁶ _____ What's three?

Ana: What language did the Romans talk in? I think it's Latin. ⁷ _____

Maria: I'm not sure. But I think they talked in Latin.

WRITING

1 Read the story. Match the questions (a–f) with the paragraphs (1–6).

Old Lord Stewart

¹Stewart Castle was old and dark. Inside the castle there were a lot of pictures of the Stewart family.

²One afternoon, two girls arrived at the castle. They were on holiday in the village and they wanted to see the pictures.

³First the girls walked upstairs. They talked and laughed and looked at the pictures. There was a big picture of old Lord Stewart in 1812. His hair was grey and his face was serious.

⁴Then suddenly there was an old man at the top of the stairs. He was angry. He shouted 'You laughed at me!'

⁵'We didn't laugh at you!' the girls said. 'We're just visiting the castle.' The old man said 'Well, I don't like it. It's my castle,' and he started to walk down the stairs. Suddenly all the lights went out. It was very dark. The girls were afraid.

⁶Finally, one of the girls found a door and opened it. In the light they saw the picture of Lord Stewart again – it was the old man. Was he really a ghost? The girls didn't know, but they ran from the castle very, very fast!!

a What happened next? _____
b What did the girls say? _____
c What happened in the end? _____
d Where did the story happen? *1*
e What happened first? _____
f Who arrived? _____

2 Complete the sentences. Decide if the girls or Old Lord Stewart were speaking. Choose the correct verb and punctuation.

1 Where are the pictures?
 The girls / Old Lord Stewart *asked* / said / shouted 'Where are the pictures*?* / !'

2 You laughed at me!
 Old Lord Stewart / The girls shouted / asked / said 'You laughed at me! / ?'

3 What are you doing here?
 Old Lord Stewart / The girls asked / said / shouted 'What are you doing here? / .'

4 We're just visiting your castle.
 The girls / Old Lord Stewart said / asked / shouted 'We're just visiting your castle. / ?'

5 It's my castle.
 Old Lord Stewart / The girls said / asked / shouted 'It's my castle. / ?'

6 Help!
 The girls / Old Lord Stewart shouted / asked / said 'Help! / .'

3 Read the story. Choose the correct words to complete the plan for the end of the story.

1 They *walked* / on downstairs: nobody there.
2 Sonia: 'Maybe / Never it was a ghost!'
3 Door closed with / behind them.
4 Alex: 'Come / Let's go!'
5 Went to / out their car.
6 Of / In the end – an interesting day!

Alex and Sonia went to Ireland on holiday. On the second day of the holiday they visited a castle in Cork. That morning they travelled to the castle in their car.

At lunchtime they stopped the car. They had some sandwiches. They looked at the information in their guidebook and talked about the castle. 'The castle is 600 years old!' Sonia said.

In the afternoon they arrived at the castle. They walked upstairs and looked out of the windows. Then Alex saw an old man downstairs. 'Hello!' he shouted, 'Can you tell us about the castle?' The man didn't look at him. 'Perhaps he can't hear me,' Alex said.

4 Write the end of the story, using the plan and your own ideas. Use words to show the order of events. Remember to use speech marks (' ') when Alex or Sonia speak.

08 Young people, big ideas!

VOCABULARY
Common verbs

1 Match the pictures with these verbs, then write the past simple forms.

~~buy~~   give   sing   study   win   write

1
buy
bought

2
....
....

3
....
....

4
....
....

5
....
....

6
....
....

2 Complete the table.

Infinitive	Past simple form
1) find	found
2)	went
3)	learned
4)	left
5)	said
6)	saw

3 Match the verbs (1–6) with the past simple forms (a–f).

1 become   a turned
2 have   b made
3 make   c became
4 start   d wanted
5 turn   e had
6 want   f started

4 Choose the correct answer, A, B or C.

1 Lilka _gave_ me a picture for my birthday. She made it for me.
   A had   B saw   **C gave**
2 I _____ to play the guitar when I was seven.
   A turned   B started C found
3 We _____ the film at the cinema last Saturday.
   A saw   B made   C won
4 My mum is a good cook. She _____ a fantastic chicken salad for me yesterday.
   A wrote   B made   C became
5 The train for London _____ at 10.30.
   A left   B bought   C learned
6 The boys _____ the football match 5–1.
   A studied B wanted   C won
7 London is amazing! My cousins _____ there last July.
   A said   B went   C wanted

5 Complete the sentences with the verbs in brackets. Use the past simple form.

1 I _bought_ (buy) a guitar last week. I'm learning to play.
2 Jessica _____ (study) a lot before the exam.
3 Charles Dickens _____ (write) the book *Oliver Twist* in 1838.
4 The children were very good, they _____ (play) together all afternoon.
5 'I'm having fun!' she _____ (say).
6 I wasn't at school yesterday because I _____ (have) a temperature.

08 Young people, big ideas!

READING

1 Read the article quickly. Put the title and the paragraph headings in the correct places. There are two paragraph headings you do not need.

> What does Chris Haas say?
> Chris today   What was Chris's 'big idea'?
> ~~The Story of Chris Haas and his 'big idea'~~
> Susan's book   Who is Chris Haas?
> Becoming famous   Chris at school

1 *The Story of Chris Haas and his 'big idea'*
2 ....

Chris Haas lives in California in the USA. Chris's father was a basketball teacher. Chris learned to play basketball when he was young.

3 ....

Chris was nine years old when he had his big idea for the 'hands-on basketball'. He saw children who had problems with the basketball. This gave him the idea for a special basketball. The ball had big hands on it to help children learn to play better.

4 ....

Susan Casey wrote about Chris in her book, Kids Inventing! The book was about young people who make things. Chris said that he put the ball into a competition at school but it didn't win.

5 ....

The ball became popular though and Chris became famous! He made money for his brother and sister to study. Chris also started to help young people with other projects.

6 ....

Chris is now in his 20s. He made another ball, a 'hands-on football', for children to learn to play football. He also has two books Shooting for your Dreams and Slamming Success Stories. The 'hands-on basketball' is still popular around the world today.

2 Read the article. Choose the correct answer, A, B or C.

1 What was Chris's dad's job?
 A Basketball teacher ✓
 B Basketball player
 C Basket maker
2 How old was Chris when he had his big idea?
 A Nineteen **B** Ten **C** Nine
3 What was on the special ball?
 A Numbers **B** Pictures **C** Hands
4 Did Chris win the competition at school?
 A No, he didn't.
 B Yes, he did.
 C He doesn't remember.
5 Who did Chris help when he became famous?
 A His brother and sister.
 B His brother and sister and other young people.
 C Other young people.
6 How many books did Chris write?
 A One **B** Three **C** Two

GRAMMAR
Past simple: irregular verbs

1 Rewrite the sentences in the past simple.

1 1922: Howard Carter finds Tutankhamun's tomb.
 Howard Carter found Tutankhamun's tomb in 1922.
2 1969: Neil Armstrong goes to the moon.
 ....
3 2010: Spain win the football World Cup.
 ....
4 Around 1590: William Shakespeare writes *Romeo and Juliet*.
 ....
5 2009: Barack Obama becomes president of the USA.
 ....
6 2008: Catherine Hardwicke makes the first *Twilight* film.
 ....

2 Complete the article with the verbs in brackets in the negative past simple.

This week in **Running Wild**, Paula Clifford tells us about a running race she did across the Sahara Desert in Africa with a group of other runners.
"It was a great trip but it 1) *wasn't* (be) always fun. I was with the same ten people every day and I 2) .... (have) any time alone – sometimes we were all very tired and we 3) .... (want) to talk. We 4) .... (eat) any fresh food for a month, just pasta and rice, and I 5) .... (sleep) well in the tent. I 6) .... (know) it was cold in the desert at night and I 7) .... (have) warm clothes – I was always freezing! But the experience was amazing and we all became friends. I 8) .... (win) the race across the desert but I learned a lot about myself."

3 Read the answers. Complete the questions.

1 A: _Did_ you _see_ Mum?
B: Yes, I did. I saw her at the supermarket.
2 A: _____ you _____ the tickets?
B: No, we didn't. You have to buy them tomorrow.
3 A: _____ he _____ Helen the bag?
B: Yes, he did. He gave her the mobile phone, too.
4 A: _____ they _____ after lunch?
B: Yes, they did. They left at half past two.
5 A: _____ she _____ dinner at home?
B: Yes, she did. She had dinner with her family.
6 A: _____ you _____ a lot?
B: Yes, I did. I wrote ten pages.

4 Make questions. Use these verbs in the past simple and start with *Did*.

> arrive   play   start   ~~travel~~   walk   want

1 Yuri Gagarin / in space
  Did Yuri Gagarin travel in space?
2 Ed Stafford / along the Amazon River
  _____
3 John Lennon / the drums
  _____
4 Alejandro Sanz / playing the guitar when he was a boy
  _____
5 Kristen Stewart / to be famous
  _____
6 Maria Sharapova / in the USA when she was six
  _____

5 Choose the correct answer, A, B or C.

1 Did you leave your book at school?
  A Yes, I do.   (B) Yes, I did.
  C Yes, it did.
2 Did Clare turn off the TV?
  A No, she wasn't.   B No, she didn't.
  C No, she hasn't.
3 Did Chelsea win the football match?
  A Yes, we did.   B Yes, she did.
  C Yes, they did.
4 Did they like the salad?
  A Yes, they did.   B Yes, you did.
  C Yes, they were.

VOCABULARY
Adjectives

1 Read the clues. Rearrange the letters to make adjectives.

1 My favourite subject is English. My teacher is _good_. dgoo
2 I liked the film but it was really _____. ads
3 Sam is _____. He can help you clean that window. lalt
4 My dogs are _____ when I arrive home. pyahp
5 Meerkats stand on their legs to look around because they are _____. tohrs
6 It's _____ to find things in this room. Tidy it! fiflcudi

2 Choose the correct words.

1 I play the drums. They're very *loud/long*.
2 Stefan's got a new motorbike. He's *happy/easy*.
3 You can read in the garden. It's *slow/quiet* there.
4 Rita is a *clean/good* actor. She is on TV.
5 The talent show is for adults. Liam is a *young/short* boy, so he can't sing in it.
6 I've got a *bad/tall* cough.
7 Andrea says maths is *fast/easy*, but I don't like it.

3 Make sentences about the photos. Use four words from the box and the verb *be*.

> difficult   dirty   fast   happy   ~~old~~   tall

1
It's old.

2
_____

3
_____

4
_____

08 Young people, big ideas!

4 Read the conversation and choose the best answer, A, B or C.

Justine: Is this you in the photo? You look quite 1) *young*.
Mum: Yes, I was about 12. Oh! That was a 2) _____ day.
Justine: Was it a new bike?
Mum: Yes. My parents bought it for my birthday. It wasn't 3) _____ to ride.
Justine: It looks 4) _____.
Mum: Yes, it wasn't a very fast bike. But I loved it. It was usually 5) _____ because I cycled all around the village.
Justine: Who is that 6) _____ boy next to you?
Mum: That's your Uncle Val.
Justine: Really? He's 7) _____ in this photo.
Mum: I know. He wanted a bike, too!

1	A short	(B) young	C sad
2	A easy	B short	C happy
3	A sad	B easy	C loud
4	A slow	B happy	C clean
5	A short	B dirty	C difficult
6	A fast	B loud	C tall
7	A sad	B quiet	C bad

5 Read and solve the puzzle. Write the names of the horses.

1	*Bella*	Lightning
2		Ned
3		Bella
4		Ruby
5		Jet
6		Buddy

Lightning is a fast horse. He is between the tall horse and the bad horse. Ruby is next to the old horse. The bad horse isn't Jet. Buddy isn't tall or loud. Bella is the old horse. Jet is next to Ruby. Ned is next to the bad horse. He's loud.

LISTENING

1 🔊 8.1 Listen to the interview with Maria. Choose the best words or phrases to complete the sentences.

1 Maria and Ben's 'big idea' makes *electricity/music/food*.
2 The science competition was at Maria's *home/school/sports centre*.
3 Maria saw the electric guitar *at a museum/on the Internet/in a book*.
4 The first model *didn't work/worked/wasn't right*.
5 Ben and Maria made the guitar in *three months/a month/three weeks*.
6 The interviewer says other children want to make *a model/make a guitar/win a competition*.

2 🔊 8.2 Listen again and answer the questions. Write between one and four words.

1 Who is Ben?
   Maria's friend.
2 How old were Maria and Ben when they made the electric guitar?
   _____.
3 Who did the design for the guitar?
   _____.
4 When did they start to make the guitar?
   _____.
5 When did they finish the guitar?
   _____.
6 Did they win the competition at school?
   _____.
7 Where did Ben write about the guitar?
   _____.

GRAMMAR
Past simple: wh- questions

1 Choose the correct words.

1 *What/Where* did you go on holiday?
2 When *was/did* you finish your homework?
3 What *did/was* the teacher say?
4 *Was/Did* the music loud?
5 *When/What* did the film start?
6 Where *did/was* the party?
7 *Why/Who* didn't you buy the motorbike?

2 Choose the correct answer, A, B or C.

1. ___When___ did the bus arrive?
   A When   **B** Where   **C** How
2. _____ won the competition?
   A What   **B** Why   **C** Who
3. _____ film did you see?
   A Where   **B** What   **C** When
4. _____ didn't you say 'hello'?
   A Why   **B** What   **C** Who
5. _____ did you go on holiday?
   A Where   **B** What   **C** How
6. _____ was the food?
   A When   **B** Why   **C** How

3 Put the words in the correct order to make questions.

1. that / she / message? / did / write / Why
   Why did she write that message?
2. favourite / was / picture? / What / your
3. the / train / did / leave? / When
4. did / sister / your / to / go / school? / Where
5. did / Who / see / you / the / café? / at
6. Where / find / the / book? / did / geography / you

4 Match the questions (1–7) with the answers (a–g).

1. Where did you go with your school?
2. What did you see?
3. Who did you go with?
4. How did you find all the places?
5. What did you have for lunch?
6. Why did you go?
7. When did you arrive home?

a. To practise our English.
b. We went to London.
c. We had a map.
d. Ten students from my class.
e. We had lots of sandwiches.
f. Last Saturday.
g. We saw museums and famous places.

5 Make questions about Steven Spielberg. Use these verbs.

> be   ~~be born~~   become   learn   make
> start   study   win

Steven Spielberg

Name: Steven Spielberg
1. Born: 1946, Cincinnati, USA
2. Studied at California State University
3. Became a film-maker in 1969
4. Learned to be a film-maker at Universal Studios
5. First films: adventure films
6. Made *Jaws* in 1975
7. Won the Academy Award for *Schindler's List* in 1993
8. Started making films because he wanted to tell adventure stories

1. (Where) _Where was he born?_
2. (Where) _____
3. (When) _____
4. (Where) _____
5. (What) _____
6. (When) _____
7. (When) _____
8. (Why) _____

SPEAKING SKILLS

1 Look at the pictures of Rita's holiday. Match the questions (1–7) with the answers (a–g).

08 Young people, big ideas!

1 When did Rita go?
2 Where did Rita go?
3 How did she go there?
4 Who did she go with?
5 What did she do there?
6 Did she enjoy the holiday?
7 What was her favourite thing on the trip?

a She went to Paris.
b She went on some rides.
c She liked playing tennis best.
d She went with her mum and dad.
e She went in August.
f She went by train.
g Yes, she did.

2 Read the answers. Choose the correct word to complete the questions.

1 *Where/When* did you go? I went to Istanbul.
2 *Who/What* did you go with? With my teacher and my class.
3 *When/How* did you travel there? We went by plane.
4 What did you *eat/do*? We walked on the city walls and visited lots of things.
5 What was your favourite *thing/meal*? Visiting the Grand Bazaar market.
6 What was the *city/weather* like? It was sunny and hot.
7 Did you *take/see* a lot of photographs? Yes, I did. Here is one which shows …

WRITING

1 Read about Daniel Radcliffe. Choose the correct words.

Daniel Jacob Radcliffe ¹*is born/were born/was born* in 1989 and ²*grew up/grow up/grown up* in London. His parents were both actors when they were children. Daniel ³*is acting/liked acting/likes acting* when he was very young – just five years old – but he didn't go to acting school.

He started acting on television when he was 10 and ⁴*he makes/he made/him made* the first Harry Potter film when he was 11. I love Daniel in all the Harry Potter films, but my favourite is Harry Potter and the Philosopher's Stone.

After the Harry Potter films Daniel acted in the theatre in London. Then ⁵*he went/he goes/him went* to the USA. He acted and sang in a show in New York. The show was popular and people saw that he is a ⁶*bad actor/good teacher/good actor*.

Daniel gives money to charities. His favourite charity helps very sick children. One Christmas, he asked people to send money to this charity. He didn't want them to buy ⁷*him presents/her presents/him parties*. That's why he is a special person. He's not just famous for Harry Potter now!

2 Read a student's writing project about Usain Bolt and complete the table with one or two words in each space.

Usain Bolt
Usain Bolt is a famous sportsman. He is from Jamaica. Usain was born in 1986 and grew up in a small town called Sherwood Content.
    Usain won six Olympic gold medals in Beijing and London. People like him because he is good for sport; he is a good runner but he is funny, too.
    I think Usain is cool because he is a fantastic runner but he is real person. He likes music, dancing and football.

Where is he from?	He's from *Jamaica*.
When was he born?	He was born in _____.
Where did he grow up?	He grew up in _____.
What is his job?	He's a _____.
Why do people like Usain?	He's good for _____.
Why does the student like Usain?	He's a fantastic runner but he's a _____.

3 Complete the information about a famous person. Use sentences.

Where is he/she from? When was he/she born? Where did he/she grow up? What is his/her job? Why do people like him/her? Why do you like this person?

4 Use the example about Usain Bolt and the list of questions to help you write a project.

Revision Units 7-8

VOCABULARY

1 Rearrange the letters to make ordinal numbers. Then put the cardinal numbers.

1	rihrtd	third	3
2	tsifr		
3	ighhet		
4	thewflt		
5	txeeishtn		
6	iewenttht		
7	ytewnt-cendos		

2 Match the dates (1–6) with the way we write them (a–f).

1 the fifth of March nineteen ten
2 the fifteenth of March nineteen ninety
3 the fifth of May nineteen nineteen
4 the fifteenth of May nineteen ten
5 the fifth of March nineteen oh nine
6 the fifth of March nineteen ninety-nine

a 5 March 1999
b 5 March 1909
c 15 May 1910
d 5 March 1910
e 5 May 1919
f 15 March 1990

3 Complete the table with these verbs.

arrive at   buy   give   go to   play   sing   stay at   write

1) buy
2) ... a present
3)
4) ... a friend's house
5)
6)
7) ... a song
8)

4 Choose the correct answer, A, B or C.

1 My friend _made_ us some pasta yesterday evening.
   A saw   B made   C cleaned
2 Did you _____ your room at the weekend?
   A tidy   B travel   C arrive
3 I can't _____ my mobile phone! Where is it?
   A talk   B turn   C find
4 We _____ to the cinema last night. The film was really good.
   A won   B went   C wrote
5 Steven Spielberg _____ a film-maker when he was just 23.
   A arrived   B became   C went

5 Find and make the opposites of these adjectives.

1 difficult _easy_
2 short
3 dirty
4 loud
5 slow
6 happy

q	t	s	c	l	q	f	a	s	t
u	a	y	o	n	t	u	m	f	e
c	l	n	e	a	s	y	i	c	b
c	l	f	s	s	a	o	e	e	o
s	w	e	a	t	d	u	s	u	t
p	q	u	a	p	t	n	t	q	r
a	y	u	o	n	s	g	b	z	x

6 Complete the text. Use the opposites of the words in brackets.

Excelsior Hotel

Excelsior Hotel   Overall rating: **

This hotel is 1) (difficult) _easy_ to find. It's next to the bus station. Our room was 2) (clean) _____ and we didn't sleep because it was very 3) (quiet) _____ outside. There were 4) (not many) _____ buses. We visited in November and the hotel was 5) (hot) _____. The room service was 6) (fast) _____, too. We didn't have a 7) (bad) _____ holiday at the Excelsior.

Revision Units 7–8

GRAMMAR

1 Complete the sentences with *is*, *are*, *was* or *were*.

1. The train __was__ fast but quiet.
2. There _____ 25 people at the party yesterday.
3. Look! _____ that your brother over there?
4. The teacher _____ (not) very happy with me on Monday. I didn't do my homework.
5. It _____ (not) easy to clean a house in the past.
6. How many stairs _____ there in your house?
7. _____ you at the sports centre yesterday afternoon?

2 Complete the paragraph with these verbs. Use the past simple form.

> arrive   ~~be~~   buy   go   not stay
> study   travel   win

My grandfather 1) __was__ very young when he 2) _____ in the USA. His parents 3) _____ there from Italy to work. He 4) _____ science and he 5) _____ a prize. He 6) _____ in the USA. He 7) _____ to a lot of different countries and 8) _____ a house in Australia. Now he lives in Sydney. We usually visit him in the summer.

3 Choose the correct answer, A, B or C.

1. Did you find your bag?
   A Yes, I did.   B Yes, I do.
   C Yes, it did.
2. Was it your birthday on the fourth?
   A Yes, it is.   B Yes, it was.
   C Yes, I am.
3. Did your parents help you do your homework?
   A No, they don't.   B No, they didn't.
   C No, they weren't.
4. Did I really say that?
   A Yes, you were.   B Yes, you are.
   C Yes, you did.
5. Were the trams slow today?
   A Yes, they were.   B Yes, it was.
   C Yes, there were.
6. Were there any crisps on the table?
   A Yes, they did.   B Yes, they were.
   C Yes, there were.

4 Choose the correct words.

Interviewer: Hello, Donald. Thank you for talking to me today.
Donald: That's OK. Please call me Don.
Interviewer: My first question is why did you 1) *become/became* a singer?
Donald: Because I 2) *love/loved* singing when I was a boy.
Interviewer: And where did you 3) *learned/learn* to sing?
Donald: I didn't 4) *have/had* singing lessons. I learned from my dad.
Interviewer: When 5) *did/have* you make your first CD? Was it in 1984?
Donald: Yes. When I was 18. When I 6) *did leave/left* school.
Interviewer: Really? And did you 7) *play/played* the guitar at school?
Donald: No, I 8) *didn't/don't*. I started to play in 1988, after my second CD.

5 Read the answers and make *wh-* questions. Use the past simple.

1. Q When __did you visit Warsaw?__
   A I visited Warsaw last spring.
2. Q When _____?
   A The party was on Saturday evening.
3. Q What _____?
   A We talked about computer games.
4. Q Why _____?
   A She became a photographer because she loved taking photos.
5. Q Where _____?
   A The group's first show was in Granada.
6. Q Why _____?
   A My little sister was happy because she went to a party.
7. Q How _____?
   A They travelled to the forest by bike.

09 Head to toe

VOCABULARY
Adjectives to describe hair

1 Match the pictures with these words and phrases.

curly   long fair   ~~long wavy~~
short and straight   spiky   wavy

1 _long wavy_
2
3
4
5
6

2 Put the words in the correct order.

1 got / dark / hair. / I've / curly
I've got curly dark hair.
2 Owen's / spiky / hair. / got / short
3 long / hair. / like / I / straight
4 wants / curly / She / hair. / long
5 boy's / fair / wavy / That / got / hair.
6 got / long / red / sister's / My / hair.

3 Look and make sentences about the hairstyles. Use *have got*.

She's got long curly hair.

READING

1 Read the article on page 65 quickly and answer the questions.

1 The name of a film:
'Shakespeare in Love'
2 The names of two places in England:

3 Four jobs:
4 The name of a city in the USA:

64 GOLD EXPERIENCE

Famous twins

Some people are famous because we always see them on TV or in films. But how does it feel to be famous because your twin is famous.

A quiet life
British actor Joseph Fiennes is famous for the film 'Shakespeare in Love'. He also has a twin brother. Jacob is taller than Joseph and he's got fair hair and blue eyes. He doesn't work in the theatre or in film and he doesn't live in London. He lives in a small village in Norfolk, England. 'I'm very different from the rest of my family,' says Jacob, 'I'm a country boy and I like the quiet life.'

Music and teaching
Actor and singer Alanis Morissette has a twin brother called Wade. Wade is 12 minutes older than Alanis. He is a musician, a singer and a yoga teacher. The twins don't meet very often. They live in different countries and they travel a lot. But in 2008 Wade helped at one of Alanis's concerts. He played his music at the start of the show.

A famous address
Twin sisters Jenna and Barbara Bush lived at a famous address in Washington for eight years. Their father, George W. Bush was the president of the USA. The sisters lived at the White House at the weekends. People called Jenna and Barbara 'the First Twins'. Jenna is younger than Barbara and they don't look exactly the same. Barbara's face is longer and her hair is darker.

2 Choose the best answer to each question, A or B.

1 Does Jacob Fiennes live in London?
 A Yes, he does. **B No, he doesn't.**
2 Who is shorter, Joseph or Jacob?
 A Joseph B Jacob
3 Does Jacob want to be famous?
 A No, he doesn't. B Yes, he does.
4 Who is older, Alanis or Wade?
 A Wade B Alanis
5 Why don't Alanis and Wade meet very often?
 A Because they live in different cities.
 B Because they live in different countries.
6 Where did Wade help Alanis?
 A At her concert. B At her house.
7 How long did Jenna and Barbara Bush live at the White House?
 A Eight months. B Eight years.
8 Who has a shorter face, Barbara or Jenna?
 A Barbara B Jenna

GRAMMAR
Comparative adjectives

1 Choose the correct words.

1 The bus is usually *slower/slow* than the train.
2 English is *easy/easier* than Chinese.
3 Oranges are *good/better* for you than crisps.
4 Our computer is *old/older* than that one.
5 The supermarket is nearer *than/that* the market.
6 Pasta is *nice/nicer* than rice.
7 My new mobile phone is *smaller/small* than yours.
8 Today is sunnier *then/than* yesterday.
9 My science homework is *bad/worse* than yours.
10 Gill's hair is *curly/curlier* than Jane's.

2 Read and choose the best answer, A, B or C.

Subject: **My new house!**

Hi Nathalie,
How are you? Is your arm 1) __better__ now? We've got a new house. It's 2) _____ than the old house. It's 3) _____ to find, too, because it's next to the park. There aren't a lot of cars here, so it's 4) _____ and the house is 5) _____, too.
This house has got a big garden. Monique loves playing in it. She's 6) _____ than she was in the old house. She's four years old now, and she is 7) _____ than before! It's difficult to do my homework these days.
See you soon,
Dianne

1 A best B bigger **C better**
2 A bigger B big C biggest
3 A easier B easiest C worse
4 A louder B quieter C older
5 A curlier B cleanest C cleaner
6 A sadder B happy C happier
7 A loud B louder C quieter

3 Complete the text with these adjectives in the comparative form.

curly   good   happy   loud   short   tall   ~~young~~

My family
by Wiktor Jeziorska

Here's a photo of some of the people in my family. You can see my mum and dad behind me, and also my uncle Borys. He's dad's 1) _younger_ brother, but he's 2) .... than him. I've got two sisters. They're twins. They look the same, but Anastasia's hair is 3) .... than Ala's.
My cousin Dobry is 11. His hair is short like mine, but it's 4) .... than my hair. Marek is Dobry's little brother. In this photo, Dobry is 5) .... than Marek, but usually Marek is happy and much 6) .... than his brother. We play computer games together and Marek wins because he is 7) .... than me.

4 Make sentences. Use the adjectives in the comparative form.

1. my grandfather / my grandmother (old)
   My grandfather is older than my grandmother.
2. planes / trains (fast)
   ....
3. the kitchen / the living room (dirty)
   ....
4. your singing / my singing (bad)
   ....
5. art / maths (easy)
   ....
6. pandas / meerkats (big)
   ....

VOCABULARY
Parts of the body

1 Find and write eight parts of the body.

e	y	b	a	c	k	m	e
f	m	f	e	r	o	e	t
c	o	t	a	p	m	e	o
r	u	o	o	c	u	t	e
m	t	y	t	e	e	e	a
s	h	o	u	l	d	e	r
i	f	a	c	i	e	t	k
f	i	n	g	e	r	h	l

1 _back_   5 ....
2 ....   6 ....
3 ....   7 ....
4 ....   8 ....

2 Match the photo with these words and phrases.

fingers   knee   left hand   leg   neck
nose   ~~right hand~~

1 _right hand_   2 ....
3 ....   4 ....

5 ....   6 ....
7 ....

09 Head to toe

3 How many have you got? Complete the table with parts of the body. Use plurals if necessary.

one	two	ten
nose	knees	fingers
mouth	legs	7) _____
1) _neck_	arms	
2) _____	4) _____	
3) _____	5) _____	
	6) _____	

4 Choose the correct answer, A, B or C.

1 Ouch! My _finger_ is in the door!
   A back   B tooth   **C** finger
2 Use your _____ to help you jump.
   A shoulders   B knees   C face
3 My cousin's got a bad _____. She can't play volleyball today.
   A hand   B mouth   C nose
4 How is your _____? Can you sleep OK?
   A legs   B back   C shoulders
5 I texted a lot yesterday. My _____ are tired!
   A feet   B legs   C fingers
6 My uncle's a pilot. His _____ are very good.
   A eyes   B legs   C shoulders
7 Atishoo! Sorry, it's my _____ again! I've got a cold.
   A tooth   B nose   C face

LISTENING

1 🔊 9.1 Listen to a radio programme, *The Film Show*. Match the names and film title (1–6) with the records (a–f).

1 Richard Kiel
2 Tatum O'Neal
3 Christopher Plummer
4 Roberto Benigni
5 John Ford
6 *Modern Times Forever*

a best film-maker in Hollywood
b first man to win a Best Actor Oscar without speaking English
c longest film in the world
d tallest actor
e youngest actor to win an Oscar
f oldest actor to win an Oscar

2 🔊 9.2 Listen again. Complete the notes.

1 Richard Kiel was in James Bond films in the 1970s. He's 2 metres _eighteen_ centimetres tall.
2 Tatum O'Neal won an Oscar at the age of _____ .
3 The film was *Paper Moon*. Her _____ was also in the film.
4 Christopher Plummer won an Oscar in _____ .
5 Roberto Benigni – Best Actor in 1999 for *Life is _____* . He's from Italy.
6 John Ford had _____ Oscars for Best Director.
7 The longest film is _____ hours long.

GRAMMAR
Superlative adjectives

1 Complete the table.

adjective	superlative
easy	the easiest
1) _slow_	the slowest
big	2) _____
funny	3) _____
4) _____	the worst
sad	5) _____
good	6) _____
nice	7) _____

2 Rewrite the sentences. Use the opposites of the underlined words in the superlative form.

1. My brother's bedroom is <u>the cleanest</u> in the house.
   My brother's bedroom is the dirtiest in the house.
2. I think this is <u>the best</u> DVD I've got.
3. I've got three cousins. Rafael is <u>the shortest</u>.
4. This is <u>the saddest</u> day of my life.
5. Our classroom is <u>the hottest</u> in the school.
6. They've got three dogs. Pablo is <u>the quietest</u>.

3 Complete the sentences with these adjectives in the superlative form.

~~bad~~   fast   good   long   small   young

1. Eddie Edwards was the ____worst____ ski jumper in the world. But he was the best in Britain!
2. The AVE Talgo 350 in Spain is one of the _____ trains in Europe. It travels at 330 kilometres an hour.
3. The _____ house in Britain is in Conwy, Wales. There are only two rooms – one upstairs and one downstairs.
4. Praia do Cassino in Brazil is the world's _____ beach. It's about 240 kilometres long.
5. The _____ driver to win the Formula 1 championship was Sebastian Vettel. He was 23 years old.
6. I think Robert De Niro is the _____ actor in the world. I love all his films.

4 Complete the website with these adjectives in the superlative form.

bad   ~~cold~~   hot   nice   rainy   snowy

Moscow, Russia's beautiful capital city

Q: What's the weather like in Moscow?

A: The 1) ____coldest____ months in Moscow are January and February. The temperature is usually around -9°C. The first snow is in October and it stays until April. February 2010 was the 2) _____ month in Moscow for 40 years, with 425,000 m³ of snow.

In summer the temperature is usually about 18°C. The 3) _____ months are July and August, when the temperature can be 30°C during the day.

The 4) _____ months are July and August, with around 90mm of rain.

Q: When is the best time to visit Moscow?

A: This is a difficult question. There is something to see in every season. Maybe the 5) _____ time to visit is the beginning of spring or end of autumn, because the weather is very cloudy, cold and rainy. The 6) _____ time is in the summer or the winter.

SPEAKING SKILLS

1 Choose the correct answers to the questions, A or B.

1 Is this the fastest train in the world?
   A No, I think it is.
   (B) Yes, I think it is.
2 I think she's the best actor in the film.
   A Yes, maybe she is.
   B Yes, maybe it is.
3 English is the easiest language to learn.
   A Yes, it is.
   B I don't think.
4 He's the worst teacher in our school.
   A I think it is.
   B I think you're right.
5 Is Casa the nicest restaurant in town?
   A That's it.
   B No, I don't think it is.
6 Maybe football is better than volleyball.
   A No, it isn't.
   B Maybe is it?
7 Is your mobile phone older than mine?
   A No, I think it is.
   B No, I don't think it is.

2 Francesca and Luca are talking about a photo. Complete the conversation with these words. There are three words you do not need.

> right   he   think   is   maybe   wrong
> can   it   don't

Luca: Is ¹ _it_ a river?
Francesca: No. I ² .... it's a lake.
Luca: Yes, I think you're ³ ....
       Is it in a park?
Francesca: Yes, ⁴ .... it is. That's why there are boats and people are walking.
Luca: Hmm. Is it in London?
Francesca: No. I ⁵ .... think it is. It's very sunny.
Luca: Maybe it's in Madrid.
Francesca: Yes, I think it ⁶ ....

WRITING

1 Put the words in the correct order to make sentences from a blog.

1 some / are / photos / me. / Here / of
   Here are some photos of me.
2 do / What / you / think / this / photo? / of
   ....
3 cousin / My / like / me / in / photo. / looks / this
   ....
4 I / digital / this / my / camera. / took / photo / with
   ....
5 here / my / for / photos / Click / holiday. / of / more
   ....

2 Complete the blog about a holiday. Use one word in each space.

Welcome ¹ _to_ my blog! This is a photo of me with my brother. He doesn't ² .... like me. I've got curly fair hair and he's got dark straight hair.
   I'm ³ .... this blog to tell you about my holidays in September this year. I went to Puerto Madryn in Patagonia ⁴ .... my family. It's beautiful there, but it's colder than Buenos Aires.
   Puerto Madryn is ⁵ .... best place in Argentina to see whales. I ⁶ .... this photo from the boat. In this photo a whale is swimming ⁷ .... to us!
   There were also a few dolphins with the whales. ⁸ .... 's a photo. Look! They're playing near our boat. It's my favourite photo from the holiday.

3 Plan a blog about something you like (e.g. music, sport, films, food). Think about which photos to use in the blog. Use these ideas to help you.

Title of the blog. Things I like. Description of the photos (what, where, who is in the photo).

4 Write your blog. Use short forms (*I'm, I've got, he's/she's*). Make your blog friendly and easy to read.

10 Summer's here

VOCABULARY
Sports

1 Rearrange the letters to make sports or fun activities.

1. nisnet — *tennis*
2. aaelblbs — ....
3. gknsii — ....
4. cnaidgn — ....
5. lgyccin — ....
6. ktslbbaela — ....
7. ceahb bvlloeylal — ....

2 Complete the speech bubbles with *play* or *go*.

On holiday
We asked some teenagers about their favourite holiday activities. This is what they said …

1. We usually ___go___ skiing in the mountains in France. I love skiing!
2. I often .... tennis with my dad when we are on holiday.
3. We .... camping next to the lake every summer. It's fantastic!
4. I love to .... beach volleyball. It's my favourite sport!
5. My family don't like staying on the beach. We .... surfing or swimming.

3 Rewrite the sentences in the past simple.

1. I go dancing on Sunday.
   I went dancing on Sunday.
2. She plays tennis at the sports centre.
   ....
3. Do you play baseball on Friday?
   ....
4. They go skiing in January.
   ....
5. Do you go camping near the sea?
   ....
6. Does he play basketball at school?
   ....
7. My dog goes swimming in the river.
   ....

4 Read and choose the best answer, A, B or C.

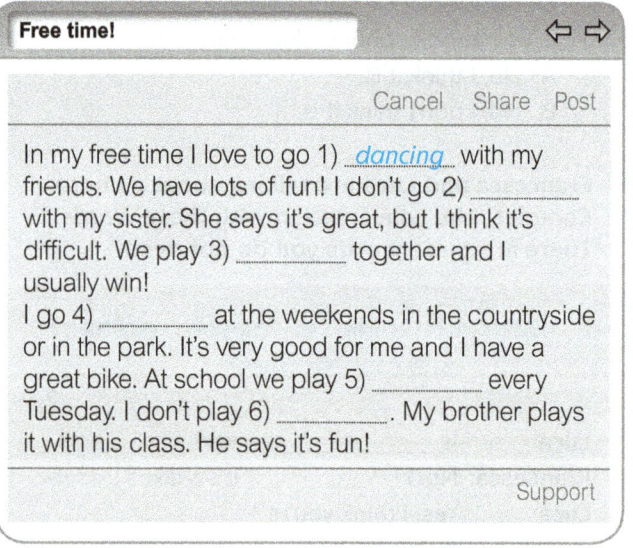

Free time!

Cancel Share Post

In my free time I love to go 1) _dancing_ with my friends. We have lots of fun! I don't go 2) .... with my sister. She says it's great, but I think it's difficult. We play 3) .... together and I usually win!
I go 4) .... at the weekends in the countryside or in the park. It's very good for me and I have a great bike. At school we play 5) .... every Tuesday. I don't play 6) .... My brother plays it with his class. He says it's fun!

Support

1. A basketball   B tennis   **C dancing**
2. A beach volleyball   B rollerblading   C baseball
3. A surfing   B hopping   C tennis
4. A cycling   B camping   C swimming
5. A skateboarding   B skiing   C basketball
6. A dancing   B baseball   C rock climbing

70 GOLD EXPERIENCE

10 Summer's here

READING

1 Read the emails and the postcard from Juan and Patricia. Answer the questions. Choose J (Juan), P (Patricia) or JP (Juan and Patricia).

1 Who is going to do sport on holiday? ...JP...
2 Who is going to visit a capital city? ....
3 Who is going to go dancing? ....
4 Who is having a great time on holiday? ....
5 Who is learning English on their holiday? ....
6 Who is planning to come back next year? ....

Hi Patricia!
How are you? The holidays start in two weeks and I'm going to go to London for a month. It's an activity holiday! You can do sports and leisure activities like swimming and tennis. You can practise speaking English, too.
I'm going to learn lots more English because there are trips with our English teachers. It's going to be difficult sometimes, but I can't wait to see London!
What are your plans for the summer?
Juan

Hi,
Wow! That sounds great! London is cool. I'm going to go to the beach with my family and some friends. We're planning to go next week. There's a lot to do there – go swimming, of course, play beach volleyball, go cycling and in the evenings go dancing. There are some places where you can go rock climbing, too. It's a beautiful place.
Enjoy London!
Patricia

Hi Patricia,
Well, here I am in London! I'm having a great time. There's a lot to see and do. Yesterday we went on the London Eye. You go up on a wheel and if you look down you can see a lot of the city. It was fun! It isn't easy speaking English all the time to the teachers, but it's great to talk to real English people!
Say hi to all the family and enjoy your holiday at the beach!
Juan

Hi Juan!
I'm having a great time here at the beach. We went swimming and cycling yesterday but we aren't going rock climbing today because it's raining. I'm going to come back next year, I love it here and I don't want to go home.
I'm planning to phone you when I get back so you can practise your English again!
Love,
Patricia

---

2 Read the emails and the postcard. Choose the correct answer, A, B or C to complete the sentences.

1 Juan is going to go to London for ...four weeks... .
   A four weeks   **B** a week   **C** two weeks
2 Juan's going to go on trips with ....
   A his family   **B** his teachers   **C** his brothers
3 Patricia is planning to go .... at the beach.
   A swimming, cycling and dancing
   B swimming, cycling and rollerblading
   C swimming, shopping and dancing
4 Juan went on the London Eye because he wanted to ....
   A see a lot of the city   **B** practise his English
   C learn about the history of the city
5 Juan says it's .... to talk to English people.
   A easy   **B** boring   **C** great
6 Patricia doesn't go rock climbing because ....
   A it's very difficult   **B** she doesn't like it
   C the weather is bad

GRAMMAR
Going to

1 Look at the photos. Make sentences with *going to*.

1 *They're going to go rollerblading.*
2 ....
3 ....
4 ....
5 ....
6 ....

71

2 Rewrite the sentences in the negative form.

1 We're going to win.
   We aren't going to win.
2 He's going to sing in the show.
3 They're going to have a party.
4 I'm going to go shopping.
5 You're going to clean your bedroom.
6 She's going to go dancing.

3 Complete the conversation with *be going to* in the correct form.

Dave: Where are you going?
Ann: To the shops in the town centre.
Dave: What 1) *are* you *going to* buy?
Ann: Some new clothes for my holiday in Australia. We 2) .... visit my aunt and uncle.
Dave: Wow! What kind of clothes do you want?
Ann: Well … My aunt and uncle live near the sea, so I 3) .... buy a swimsuit.
Dave: Good idea. 4) .... you .... get some sunglasses, too?
Ann: Yes, I am. And some shorts and T-shirts, because it 5) .... be sunny and hot.
Dave: Hmm. 6) .... n't it .... be difficult to find shorts and T-shirts in the shops? It's December!

4 Make positive (+) or negative (−) short answers.

1 Are you going to go surfing this summer? (−)
   No, I'm not.
2 Is he going to go dancing with his friends? (+)
3 Are we going to go swimming this afternoon? (+)
4 Are they going to go cycling tomorrow? (−)
5 Am I going to play basketball for the school? (+)
6 Is it going to rain at the football match? (−)

5 Make questions. Use *going to* in the correct form.

1 you / go to Disneyland in the summer
   Are you going to go to Disneyland in the summer?
2 you / travel by plane
3 the weather / be hot
4 your sister / go with you
5 you all / stay in a hotel
6 the holiday / be in the summer

VOCABULARY
Clothes

1 Look at the pictures. Complete the crossword puzzle.

1 J A C K E T

10 Summer's here

2 Write the words you can use with 'a pair of'. Use the plural form. You do not need all the words.

~~boot~~   hat   jacket
jeans   sandal   shirt
shoe   shorts   skirt
sunglasses   sweatshirt
swimsuit   tights
trainer   T-shirt

A pair of…
boots

3 Choose the correct words.

1 It's sunny. I need my *sunglasses*/*tights*.
2 It's windy. I'm wearing my *shorts*/*jacket*.
3 It's rainy. I've got my *boots*/*sandals* on.
4 It's cool. Wear your *shorts*/*jeans*.
5 It's hot. Where are my *boots*/*shorts*?
6 It's wet. Put on a *hat*/*T-shirt*.

4 Complete the sentences.

1 It's winter. I'm going to buy some b o o t s and a h a t .
2 I'm at the beach. I've got my sw_____ and my sun_____.
3 I'm going to a special party. I'm going to wear a sh_____ and a j_____.
4 I'm going to stay at home in my je_____ and sw_____.
5 I'm going to play tennis in my sh_____ and a T-_____.

5 Complete the blog with these words.

boots   sandals   ~~shirts~~   shorts
sunglasses   swimsuits

" On Saturdays I help in my parents' clothes shop. There are a lot of different clothes in our shop. There are 1) __shirts__ and jackets for special parties or sports clothes, for example 2) _____ for the pool. Our 3) _____ and T-shirts are good for going to the beach on holiday. I like the 4) _____ we've got. They are fantastic for your eyes on very sunny days. We've got shoes for different weather: 5) _____ in the summer and 6) _____ in the winter. "

LISTENING

1 🔊 10.1 Listen to Silvia, Dan, Yuli and Frederick talking about their plans for the future. Complete the table.

Name	likes / loves …	wants to …
Silvia	1 *playing tennis*	be a 2 _____ and win 3 _____
Dan	travelling in planes	be a 4 _____ when he leaves school
Yuli	living in the 5 _____	travel to 6 _____, learn about life there, study and be a Chinese 7 _____
Frederick	playing the 8 _____	be in a rock band and travel the world

2 🔊 10.2 Listen again. Complete the sentences with two words in each space.

1 Silvia doesn't 1 __like practising__ her tennis.
2 Dan doesn't want 2 _____ in an office or a shop.
3 Dan thinks being a pilot is 3 _____ job in the world.
4 Yuli doesn't want 4 _____ in China, but she wants to study there.
5 Frederick doesn't like playing 5 _____.
6 Frederick doesn't want to be 6 _____.

GRAMMAR
Want + to + infinitive, Like/Love + -ing

1 Choose the correct words.

1 What do you want *doing*/*to do* on holiday?
2 We love *play*/*playing* tennis in the summer.
3 Francesco and Sergio want *to go*/*going* shopping.
4 My brother likes *playing*/*play* basketball.
5 I want *to go*/*going* camping.
6 What does Beata like *do*/*doing* at the weekends?
7 We like *live*/*living* by the sea because we can swim every day.
8 The children want to *have*/*having* a bigger bedroom.

2 Complete the sentences with the correct form of these verbs, in the infinitive or –ing form.

> be   go   listen   play   stay   tidy   watch

1 My cousin wants ___to be___ a dancer.
2 I don't like _____ my bedroom.
3 Does your friend want _____ to some music with us?
4 My sister loves _____ TV in the afternoon.
5 I don't like _____ dancing with my parents.
6 Do you want _____ at home in the holidays?
7 The students love _____ computer games at lunchtime.

3 Choose the correct answer, A, B or C.

1 What time do you want ___to go___ shopping?
  A going   B to go   C to want
2 Stella loves _____ skiing.
  A to play   B playing   C going
3 We want _____ English every day!
  A to study B learning C studying
4 My parents like _____ to France on holiday.
  A to go   B travelling C to travel
5 Do you want _____ a basketball player?
  A learning B to learn C to be
6 I love _____ my friends after school.
  A to study B to meet   C meeting

4 Put the conversation in the correct order.

Maria: But you love playing sport. You can study sports science at university. ___
Maria: Yes, I do. I want to be a doctor. I like studying science. ___
Kara: No, I don't … but I don't want to go to university. I don't like studying! ___
Kara: Yes, that's true. I like going swimming and playing football. What about you? You don't like playing sports. Do you know what you want to be? ___
Kara: A doctor? That's fantastic. ___
Maria: Do you know what you want to study after school? ___1___

5 Read the notes and the text about James. Complete the text about Alex with verbs in the infinitive or -ing form.

💬 View previous comments   Cancel   Share   Post

Name: James
Home town: Cambridge
Age: 14
Likes: computer games, guitar lessons
Dislikes: shopping, skiing
Favourite subject: science
Favourite job: pilot
Dream: visit Africa

💬 View previous comments   Cancel   Share   Post

Name: Alex
Home town: Manchester
Age: 15
Likes: tennis, travel
Dislikes: TV, swimming
Favourite subject: art
Favourite job: photographer
Dream: write a book

James likes playing computer games. He likes having guitar lessons. He doesn't like going shopping or going skiing. His favourite subject is science. He wants to be a pilot and he wants to visit Africa.

Alex likes 1) ___playing___ tennis and he likes 2) _____ . He doesn't like 3) _____ TV or 4) _____ swimming. His favourite subject is art. He wants 5) _____ a photographer and he wants 6) _____ a book one day.

SPEAKING SKILLS

1 Put the lines of the conversation in the correct order (1–8).

Pierre: I see. You don't want to see two films this weekend. ___
Marie: Hi, Pierre! What do you want to do this weekend? ___1___
Pierre: Yeah! That sounds great. ___
Marie: OK. Good idea! I love going rollerblading. ___

10 Summer's here

Marie: I'm not sure about going this evening. I'm planning to go to the cinema on Sunday night with my sister. ___

Pierre: Good. Rollerblading on Saturday. Let's go to the cinema this evening. ___

Pierre: Hello, Marie! I'm not sure … What about going rollerblading with André and Santine on Saturday? ___

Marie: No, I don't. What about going dancing? ___

2 Choose the correct words to complete the telephone conversation.

Lukasz: Hi, Justina. What are you going to do this weekend? ¹*Who/Why/What* about going shopping on Saturday morning?

Justina: OK. Good ²*idea/morning/right*, Lukasz! I haven't got any plans for Saturday morning.

Lukasz: And ³*let's go/can go/we are* going to go to the cinema in the evening.

Justina: Mmm. What about ⁴*are going/going/go to* Leon's party? It starts at seven o'clock. You love parties.

Lukasz: Yes, I do. That ⁵*looks/seems/sounds* great!

Justina: I'm going to go on a nature walk on Sunday with Sofia. Come with us.

Lukasz: I'm ⁶*being/not/never* sure. I'm going to go swimming with my brother on Sunday.

Justina: OK. See you on Saturday morning, then.

Lukasz: Yes. See you then.

WRITING

1 Complete Karen's notes about her holiday plans with these verbs. There are three verbs you do not need.

> go   walk   talk   take   have
> visit   ~~play~~   make   meet

- **Friday 21st**
  morning: ¹ _play_ tennis
  afternoon: ² _____ the Roman museum
- **Saturday 22nd**
  morning: ³ _____ swimming
  afternoon: ⁴ _____ Sandra at the beach
- **Sunday 23rd**
  ⁵ _____ lunch at Café Bruno
  afternoon: ⁶ _____ on the beach

2 Imagine you are Karen writing a postcard on Saturday to your parents. Use the notes to complete the postcard. Use *going to* to write about plans.

> Saturday 22nd July
>
> Dear Mum and Dad,
>
> I'm having a great time in Cornwall. It's Saturday morning and I'm writing this postcard at my breakfast table in the hotel.
>
> Yesterday morning ¹ _I played tennis_ with Carla. I didn't win, but I had a lot of fun.
>
> In the afternoon ² _____ in the town centre. It was really interesting.
>
> This morning ³ _____ and in the afternoon ⁴ _____ at the beach. It's a sunny day today, so we're going to play beach volleyball. I can't wait!
>
> Tomorrow ⁵ _____ at Café Bruno. My friends told me the fish is very nice there. Then in the afternoon ⁶ _____ on the beach for a while. The last walk before I come home!
>
> See you on Monday.
>
> Lots of love,
>
> Karen

3 Put the parts of this postcard in the correct order.

> Hi Louis, _1_
>
> Love Margaret _____
>
> Tomorrow I'm going to go to the zoo at 'Casa de Campo'. There are more than 3,000 animals there! _____
>
> Today it's sunny. I'm going around the city on a bus. _____
>
> I'm having a great time in Madrid. Yesterday I went to the Retiro Park. I went in a boat on the lake and played football. _____
>
> I can't wait! _____
>
> See you soon, _____
>
> It was a lot of fun. _____

4 You're away on an activity holiday. Write a postcard to your friend.

Revision Units 9 – 10

VOCABULARY

1 Complete the sentences.
1. I've got a problem with my left s_houlder_.
2. She's got long, w_____ hair.
3. Wash your h_____ before you have lunch.
4. Yuri's hair isn't the same as his brother's. It's f_____, not dark.
5. Is your little f_____r OK now?
6. Dad's got a bad l_____ because he played football yesterday.
7. My best friend's got curly hair, but she wants s_____t hair.

2 Label the picture with these clothes words.

boot   jacket   ~~jeans~~   sandal   shirt
shorts   skirt   trainer

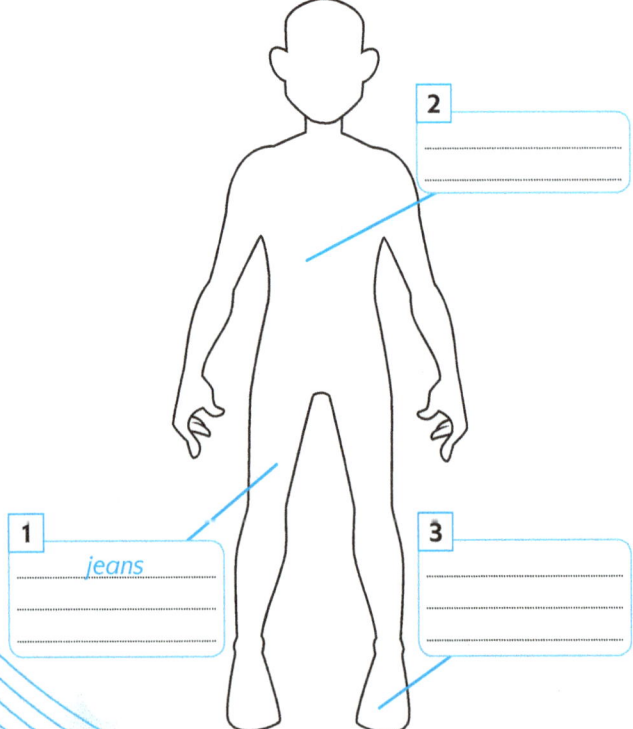

1. jeans
2.
3.

3 Match (1–7) with (a–g) to make clothes and sports words.

1. volley   a blading
2. skate   b ing
3. sun   c suit
4. sweat   d boarding
5. roller   e ball
6. swim   f glasses
7. ski   g shirt

4 Find and write four fun activities and four parts of the body.

s	h	o	l	t	n	s	z	t
h	y	d	i	e	o	h	p	e
e	h	c	a	n	s	o	a	n
k	a	n	y	n	u	p	t	n
t	n	f	o	i	c	p	i	h
a	d	e	i	s	r	i	e	a
k	n	l	e	n	e	n	n	w
c	y	c	l	i	n	g	s	g

1. tennis   5. _____
2. _____   6. _____
3. _____   7. _____
4. _____   8. _____

5 Complete the conversation.

A: It's cold today, don't you think?
B: Yes. I need a 1) h_a__t_.
A: I'm glad I've got my 2) t_____ on with this skirt, but my 3) h_____ are cold.
A: Would you like to go to the beach?
B: Yes, but I haven't got my 4) s_____t.
A: That's OK. We can wear 5) s_____s and 6) T-_____. It's a bit windy for swimming, anyway.

REVISION Units 9 – 10

GRAMMAR

1 Choose the correct answer, A, B or C.

1 Cycling is _faster_ than walking.
   A slower   B fast   **C faster**
2 These sunglasses are _____ than my old sunglasses.
   A nice   B nicer   C nicest
3 He didn't want _____ shopping with us on Saturday.
   A to go   B going   C go
4 Yolanda loves _____ beach volleyball on holiday.
   A play   B playing   C plays
5 Writing a text is _____ than writing an email.
   A difficult   B easiest   C easier
6 That's _____ café in the town centre.
   A bad   B worse   C the worst
7 Do you like camping or _____ in a hotel?
   A staying   B to stay   C stay
8 _Memories_ is _____ song on the CD.
   A sadder   B the saddest   C sad

2 Read about Emilie's friends. Put the correct names under the photographs.

> Anna's got the curliest hair. Heidi's hair is the longest. Isabel hasn't got the shortest hair and she hasn't got straight hair. Marta's hair is shorter than Jana's and Eva's hair. Eva's mouth is bigger than Jana's mouth.

 1   2

Anna

 3   4

 5  6

3 Complete the sentences. Use the correct form of _going to_ and these verbs.

| ~~be~~ | fly | go | have | play | see | watch |

1 My mum _'s going to be_ happy when she sees my bedroom. It's clean!
2 I _____ a shower before I go to the party.
3 It's not very near here. We _____ by car. The train is easier.
4 _____ Cristian _____ card games with us tomorrow?
5 There aren't any good programmes on tonight. I _____ TV.
6 _____ the bats _____ near us in the cave?
7 He _____ his favourite band in concert on Saturday night.

4 Make questions. Use the verbs in the correct form (infinitive or _-ing_).

1 you / like / go / to the beach
   Do you like going to the beach?
2 your dad / like / make lunch / on Sunday
3 Helena / want / learn / French
4 pandas / like / swim
5 your parents / want / go / camping this year
6 you / like / play / basketball

5 Complete the blog with one word in each space.

Hi! I'm Antonio. I live near the sea and I'm happy because I 1) _like_ swimming. I often go to the beach and I love 2) _____ my friends there. It's fun. We think it's much 3) _____ than staying at home. We don't like 4) _____ computer games or card games. They're boring! I want 5) _____ be a swimming teacher so I have to practise my swimming every day. It's 6) _____ to swim in a swimming pool, because it's warmer and there's no wind. But I love 7) _____ in the sea. I'm 8) _____ to go swimming at the beach now!

77

NOTES

NOTES

Pearson Education Limited
Edinburgh Gate
Harlow
Essex CM20 2JE
England
and Associated Companies throughout the world.

www.english.com/goldxp

© Pearson Education Limited 2016

The right of Lucy Frino to be identified as author of this Work has been asserted by her in accordance with the Copyright, Designs and Patents Act 1988.

All rights reserved; no part of this publication may be reproduced, stored in a retrieval system, or transmitted in any form or by any means, electronic, mechanical, photocopying, recording, or otherwise without the prior written permission of the Publishers.

First published 2016

ISBN: 9781292159454

Set in 10pt Mixage ITC Std

The publisher would like to thank the following for their kind permission to reproduce their photographs:

(Key: b-bottom; c-centre; l-left; r-right; t-top)

123RF.com: 17, 38; **Alamy Images:** Ned Bennett 68tr, Beyond Fotomedia GmbH 71tr/2, Clearview 34/6, Cultura Creative 32/5, David Noton Photography 32/2, Design Pics Inc 22bl/7, Matt Ellis 36cl/3, Eric Gevaert 36tl/1, Hero Images Inc. 58bl/3, George H.H. Huey 22br/8, Ingram Publishing 31tr, Ilene MacDonald 16tl, Francisco Martinez 44tl/1, Maged Michel 24tr/2, Keith Morris 44bl/5, 44br/6, OJO Images Ltd 16br, Parker Photography 64cl/3, Paul Mayall Australia 24tl/1, Prisma Bildagentur AG 16tr, Radius Images 32/4, Mike Rex 12, Chris Rout 44cl/3, 44cr/4, Alex Segre 32/6, Adrian Sherratt 46t/1, Tom Wood 58br; **Bahamas Tourist Office:** 22br/6; **BananaStock:** 64tl/1; **Corbis:** MM Productions 58cr/2, Ocean 53bl, Albert Pena 66, Wavebreak Media 46/3; **Digital Stock:** 23t; **Digital Vision:** 22bl/5; **DK Images:** 48bc/6, Bonetti 28, Gerard Brown 71cl/3, Terry Carter 23b, Claire Cordier 34/3, Andy Holligan 22tr/4, Dave King 13cr/D, Jamie Marshall 24cr/4, Ian O'Leary 48tl/1, Stephen Oliver 36bl/5, Gary Ombler 22tl/3, Anthony Pidgeon 13cl/C, Helena Smith 10bc/5, James Tye 34/5; **FLPA Images of Nature:** Minden Pictures / Rene Krekels 24br/6; **Fotolia.com:** Africa Studio 48br/7, andersphoto 11cl/4A, ArTo 11tl/2A, CandyBox Images 47b, Jacek Chabraszewski 31t, Les Cunliffe 34/2, Dalibor 22tl/1, Dezperado 36tr/2, Elnavegante 69br, Sonya Etchison 71tl/1, Farina3000 69tr, hitdelight 27tc, David Hughes 58cl/1, JZhuk 11cl/3A, Vitaly Krivosheev 27tr, Pavel Losevsky 7tr, Mango Stock 47t, Uroš Medved 11tr/2B, Michael Jung 13bl/E, Michael Mill 24cl/3, Andreas Mueller 11cr/3B, Claudia Nagel 44tr/2, Duncan Noakes 69bl, Photosvac 24bc/5, poligonchik 11bl/5A, William Richardson 11tr/1B, RichG 32/1, rolero54 48tc/3, Silverjohn 26cl, Ferenc Szelepcsenyi 32/3, Tatty 11cr/4B, Taxiberlin 36cr/4, tps55 25, VRD 27tl, Contrast Werkstatt 45; **Getty Images:** Amriphoto 71cr/4, John Borthwick 71br/6, Nancy R. Cohen 71bl/5, Image Source 15tr, iStock Vectors 36br/6, Carey Kirkella 16bl, Kondo Photography 64br/6, Steve Margala 64bl/5, Peter Muller 54t, Trinette Reed 10br/6, Sheer Photo 10tr/3, Taxi 4c, Tim Whitby 60; **Imagestate Media:** 34/7; **Pearson Education Ltd:** Jon Barlow 41, 74b, Gareth Boden 15tl, MindStudio 34/1, Jules Selmes 31b, 32/7, Studio 8 21b, 46b/4; PhotoDisc: 22tr/2, 48tc/2, Andrew Ward 13tl/A; **Photolibrary.com:** Nicole Goddard 74t; **Shutterstock.com:** 39, Artazum and Iriana Shiyan 11br/5B, Blessings 6, Bloomua 33b, Breadmaker 11br/6B, Carlos Caentano 11tl/1A, Claudio Divizia 32/8, Creatista 5t, Kitty 19, Krivosheev Vitaly 29, Leungchopan 24bl, Littleny 67, Mostphotos 11br, NatalieJean 26b, Natalyak 53br, Nicemonkey 13br/F, Pavel Shynkarou 11br/6A, Poznyakov 7b, Pressmaster 5c, Rob Bryon 13tr/B, thelefty 61; **Sozaijiten:** 34/4, 48tr/4, 48bl/5; **SuperStock:** 4tl, 4tr, 10tl/1, 10tc/2, 10bl/4, 46/2, 64tr/2; **www.imagesource.com:** 64cr/4, 68b

Illustrated by: Adz (Sylvie Poggio) 8l, 20tl, 42l, 49l, 66, 77; Clive Goodyer (Beehive Illustration) 17, 20br, 38, 39tl, 48; Caron Painter (Sylvie Poggio) 39bl, 63r, 72, 76; Simon Stephenson (NB Illustration) 6, 10, 52, 59; Ned Woodman 8r, 14, 28, 35, 42r, 56, 64

Cover images: *Front:* **Corbis:** Ocean

All other images © Pearson Education

Every effort has been made to trace the copyright holders and we apologise in advance for any unintentional omissions. We would be pleased to insert the appropriate acknowledgement in any subsequent edition of this publication.